What is *Christian*
in
Christianity?

What is *Christian* in Christianity?

Collected Works
by
Msgr. Lorenzo M. Albacete

HAB
Human Adventure Books

Albacete, Lorenzo.
What is Christian in Christianity? / Collected Works
First Edition

Foreword
Carl Anderson

Editorial Collaborators
Michael Carvill
Olivetta Danese
Maureen Rooney
Stephen Sanchez

Copy Editor
Melissa Massy

Cover Art
Patrick Tomassi

ISBN
978-1-941457-17-7

Contents

Foreword

By *Carl Anderson*
Supreme Knight of the Knights of Columbus

My wife and I first met Msgr. Lorenzo Albacete when we were preparing for our senior year at university and he his fourth year in seminary. We both had spent time with faculty who took their Catholic faith seriously. What we had not encountered until we met Lorenzo was someone who was thoroughly infused with the joy of the Gospel. I don't remember Lorenzo ever talking about that dimension of the Christian life; he just lived it, and lived it in a way for all to see. This was all the more remarkable amidst the controversy, division, and anger that marked the years immediately following the Second Vatican Council.[1]

Lorenzo's joy was not a result of his somehow being able to compartmentalize his life away from the hard realities of everyday living. Indeed, the opposite

---

1 Documents of the Second Ecumenical Council of the Vatican; Constitutions, Declarations, and Decrees; 1962-1965; http://www.vatican.va/archive/hist_councils/ii_vatican_council/index.htm

was the case. We always had the feeling that nothing we could say would really shock Lorenzo. He was always ready to take on all questions about and all criticisms of Christianity, and he would often respond in ways we would least expect. He was interested in the questions people really had rather than those we might wish they had. He was able to join a discussion where people lived because that is also where he lived.

He did not avert his eyes from the hard realities that so many find themselves encountering day in and day out; including the reality of suffering.

We should say, *especially* in regard to the reality of suffering. Suffering was never an abstraction for him. To the contrary, it demanded a very personal engagement. Consider what he wrote in his book, *God at the Ritz*:

"We must establish that solidarity, risk our own faith and identity, make a human connection with the sufferer, and cry out to God together. Authentic suffering, then, is a dialogue, not only with God but also among humans. To co-suffer is to share the question 'why,' to be a companion, and to walk together toward transcendence. The one who does not co-suffer and is not prepared to do so cannot speak about suffering. Such a person does not know the truth and does not speak the truth."[2]

For Lorenzo, there was no real understanding of suffering without the personal commitment of accompaniment. Indeed, accompaniment could be said to be the leitmotif

---

2 Albacete, Lorenzo; God at the Ritz: Attraction to Infinity; New York City; Crossroad Publishing Company; 2007; p. 101

of his priestly ministry. The drama of the Christian life was a daily experience for him. He lived his priestly vocation with a transparency that said, "With you I am a Christian; for you I am a priest." Often when we listened to Lorenzo respond to a difficult question we knew that he had personally worked through the same difficulty. And he conveyed that approach in the retreats he gave to priests. For example, in 2008 he said:

"So how do I know what I want? I don't know. To be with Jesus.... I don't know ultimately how this is related to me, to my fundamental and original desires. You can try to go deeper and deeper in a very noble way but, in the end, I must tell you that I find only one thing: I just want to have a good time. Yes. I don't suspect I'm lying when I say that. When I say, 'I want a life of love and justice!' That's fine. But it's more. And I am told and helped and trained to listen to myself. You yourself are the first person you minister to. How do I listen to my heart? In life there are so many adjustments, so many compromises; you seek so many distractions, undergo so many resignations. You don't have the power to cut through all that and find the original desires of your heart. I cannot. That would really be the most honest answer..."[3]

Lorenzo would tell those priests that we must live that question as a condition for helping others truly encounter Christ. With Lorenzo we knew that he was a priest *for us*, because he was

---

3 Communion and Liberation, Priests Retreat March 24-28, 2008; Lecture by Lorenzo Albacete; p. 99

also a Christian *with us*—striving with the demands of Christian discipleship in many of the same ways that we were as well. At the root of this approach to ministry was a deep humility; there was no room for the self-important. At the same time there was a deep confidence of faith that allowed for a transparency into the drama of his own religious journey.

Lorenzo was always rooted in the concrete. Perhaps this was a lasting effect of having obtained a degree in Space Science and Applied Physics before entering seminary. He often reminded us that the Christian life is based on the encounter with Christ in the flesh of our circumstances, or else it becomes pure abstraction, pure theory, and pure speculation. And, of course, this was just one reason for the remarkable relationship between Lorenzo and Don Luigi Giussani and the community of Communion and Liberation; a relationship that would providentially be so extraordinarily fruitful.

"For us, reality is clouded and our eyes search for the light that gives it meaning," writes Don Giussani in *The Journey to Truth Is an Experience*. "But only by listening and by opening oneself to the world and to that light, by becoming sensitive to the former and receptive to the latter, can one understand that that Light is true. The great adventure of human life is to reiterate that Man's proposal and to verify it."

The great adventure of Lorenzo's life was precisely this experience to reiterate Christ's proposal and to verify it in his own life. Those of us who knew him understood that this was the great adventure he was calling us to join him in. In the pages that follow, Lorenzo continues to invite us to join him and to provide us with his guidance. We should all be grateful to Olivetta Danese with the Albacete Forum and especially to Fr. Michael Carvill, Editorial Advisor to Human Adventure Books, for making this collection available to us.

Why This Book?

By Stephen Sanchez

If you were to peruse the aisles of Barnes and Noble (or Kramer's Books in Washington, D.C., as Msgr. Lorenzo Albacete was wont to do) it would be difficult not to be struck by the sheer vastness of the books that cover the topic of religion. "Scholars, mystics, charlatans, and even frauds are cashing in on the Mystery," as Lorenzo used to say, "Why not me?" Yet, in his life Msgr. Albacete only produced one book that was sold widely to the public. *God at the Ritz*[1] was a great book, but as anyone who read it would likely tell you, one book by the Mystical Monsignor could hardly be enough.

Now, as the Monsignor has joined God (though always "the Mystery" to Monsignor) in his fullness, it remains the task of his friends to make sense of a rather vast and disorganized treasury of articles, notes, retreats, speeches, homilies, letters, and (quite frankly) dinner napkins, so that we can continue

---

1 Albacete, Lorenzo; God at the Ritz: Attraction to Infinity; New York City; Crossroad Publishing Company; 2007

13

to share with posterity the unique contribution that he has made to the Church and to our lives.

Those of us that knew him all have countless stories of how he, winning us over with his wit, humor, or even sometimes desperation, would lead us down a path of profound wonder and awe that God has become flesh and so nothing could ever be the same in this world. His childhood friends could tell you about the time that Lorenzo, wrapped in a white sheet, stood in the middle of his high school courtyard on the Feast of the Ascension of the Lord with his arms stretched up to Heaven saying loudly, "I'm ready Father, your son is ready." Young Lorenzo had a flair for the dramatic, but even in his youth he had a profound sense of what was at stake in the Christian claim: It is either true, for each of us, and it changes everything or "let's pack it all up and go to the movies."

And so, a few of his friends have decided to start this task of putting together the Monsignor's works precisely with the question that he had so deliberately provoked in us. *"What is Christian in Christianity?"* is a book that draws together a collection of writings that attempt to broaden for the reader the sense of the profound Mystery that lies at the heart of Christianity:

"The smallest reality already contains within it this promise. If you look with simplicity of heart, everything that is real is a promise, a promise to your heart, a promise that your heart recognizes and pursues."[2]

---

2 Community and Liberation; Ministers of an Event: Notes from a Priest Retreat; Lecture by Lorenzo Albacete; 2006; p.22

Asking, "What is *Christian* in Christianity?" is by no means an attempt at an exhaustive list of doctrines, or dogmas, or examples. In fact, any such attempt at that kind of book would likely result in Msgr. Albacete coming back to haunt us, as he had threatened before. Instead, the path of this book means to show that this question touches upon all aspects of life: science, culture, education, love, marriage, vocation, sanctity, death, and freedom. As Monsignor Albacete says, "Because in a sense you can say, 'All life wants life.'"

For the Monsignor, no aspect of life could avoid the inevitably profound religious question that we must answer for ourselves: "What is it all for?" In answering this question, Monsignor Albacete knew that each person had to verify a claim and come to a conclusion freely and honestly. As he tells his newly baptized godson in the essay *Christianity according to Monsignor*, "whatever I have said today in your name, I have said with the understanding that you will in the future either ratify or reject it, after examining the evidence."

"*What is Christian in Christianity?*" is a book that hopes to provide the reader with a picture of what it means to walk a path of ratification. It offers a unique, and dare we say necessary, viewpoint for understanding how faith can be relevant in today's culture to anyone; young or old, Christian, or otherwise. This book walks a path of reflection and depth that we hope those who were familiar with Msgr. Lorenzo Albacete will recognize, for it is certainly one that some of us walk with him still.

Who is Lorenzo Albacete?

By Cardinal Sean O'Malley, Archbishop of Boston
Mass of Christian Burial
On the Occasion of Msgr. Lorenzo Albacete's Death
October 28, 2014

Allow me first of all to tender my heartfelt condolences to Manuel, to Mary and Olivetta, to the many friends and the CL (Communion and Liberation) communities.

I spoke with Cardinal Wuerl yesterday; he wanted to be here and sends regards and assurances of prayers and condolences. The Cardinal has asked Fr. Lee Fangmeyer and Fr. Frank Early to represent him and the archdiocese of Washington. Fr. Lorenzo was very proud to be a member of the clergy of Washington.

I also wish to express gratitude to the Parish of St. Mary's where for many years Fr. Lorenzo celebrated the Spanish mass. Thank you, Fr. Andrew, for your gracious hospitality.

We are also pleased that Archbishop Roberto Gonzalez, such a close friend of Fr. Lorenzo's, Bishop Cisneros,

Fr. Jose Medina, and Fr. Chris Marino are all with us this morning. We are especially pleased that the supreme Knight Carl Anderson and his dear wife Dorian are here as well.

"Harto difícil resulta para mi..."
(This is very hard for all of us who love this man.)

These were the opening words of my homily at Lorenzo's first Mass. They became sort of a code that I would throw into a talk if Lorenzo was present. That would always get a rise out of him. But today these words ring true: *Harto difícil resulta para mi.*

This is very hard for all of us who love this man.

Graham Greene, Evelyn Waugh, and Garcia Marquez together did not have enough imagination and genius to invent Fr. Lorenzo Albacete Cintrón. Only God could create a Lorenzo and then He broke the mold because the world did not deserve to have two Lorenzos.

In the world of Great Britain, the day after Christmas is boxing day, a day when employees and tradesmen would receive gifts. If Puerto Rico had a boxing day it would be the day after the feast of the Epiphany or "Reyes" as the Boricuas say; it would be January 7. That is the day Lorenzo arrived in this world.

He has truly been a gift, a gift of the Magi to borrow the title from O'Henry's story, but Lorenzo is the gift of the Magi, the Reyes. He has certainly been a gift in my life for almost five decades. I met Lorenzo at that time in his life when he took his famous vacation to Bogota, Colombia. A vacation Manolo arranged for Lolo (for Lorenzo). Later Lorenzo told us how he disguised himself as a priest to get near Pope John Paul. When he confessed to the pope, he was not really a priest, Blessed Pope John Paul said: "Why don't you become a priest?"

It was also around that time when Lorenzo first met Cardinal O'Boyle the Archbishop of Washington. Lorenzo and I spent a lot of time at St. Matthews Cathedral where I was working with Rosario Corredera and the Hispanic community. Lorenzo used to drive me very often. One day, as he was wont to do, Lorenzo parked in the Cardinal's parking space... (Any 'no parking' sign was an invitation to Lorenzo.) At that moment Cardinal O'Boyle was approaching and he confronted Lorenzo: "Who are you?" he asked. Lorenzo replied: "I am the Cardinal." Cardinal O'Boyle, who was something of a curmudgeon, answered back: "I am the Cardinal!" To which Lorenzo said: "Yes, you are the day Cardinal; I am the night Cardinal."

It is no wonder that after his first Mass, Lorenzo's mother asked me to bless her new apartment. I said, "But, doña Conchita, your son was just ordained." She said, "Yes, padre, but I think he is joking."

Sometimes Lorenzo ruffled the feathers of the hierarchy.

Cardinal Hickey installed a special phone with an answering machine for priests so that a priest could call it any time if he had a problem. Lorenzo used to call and say things like: "Your Eminence, I've lost my car keys, could you help me find them?" After the Cardinal was convinced that Lorenzo was not a mental case, he made him his theological advisor.

When Lorenzo was working in Boston, he bought a car phone. Only the president of the Unites States, the chief of police, and the head of the mafia had a car phones in those days. When Lorenzo had a car phone installed, I chided him for his extravagance and warned him that the auxiliary Bishop was very critical of Lorenzo's spending habits. So, Lorenzo said: "Really? Let's call him up." So Lorenzo called the Bishop from his phone in the car and said: "I'm out for a ride with Bishop Sean and I'm calling you on my new car phone. Whoops. I have to hang up, my other car phone is ringing now."

Likewise, in Boston when Lorenzo was asked to preach one of the Seven Last Words for the Good Friday services at the Cathedral of the Holy Cross, Lorenzo said: "Which of the seven last words am I supposed to speak on?" When he was told that he should preach on: "My God, my God, why have you forsaken me?" Lorenzo replied: "Good, I won't have to prepare."

And when he was installed as the Rector Magnifico of the Pontifical Catholic University of Puerto Rico, he was standing next to me on the stage. Lorenzo was wearing a baby blue academic gown with royal-blue velvet panels in the ample sleeves, a colorful hood on his back, and a velvet bonnet with a golden tassel. He was carrying something that looked like a wand. Lorenzo turned to me and said: "If this gig as president doesn't work out, I could get a job with Walter Mercado." (Mercado is a very flamboyant Puerto Rican psychic and astrologer with a Liberaci-esque wardrobe.) Lorenzo's friendship with John Paul II dates to when the then Cardinal Wojtyla visited Washington. Cardinal Baum asked Lorenzo to drive the future pope around. After he returned to Poland, Cardinal Wojtyla wrote to Lorenzo with comments and ideas on the research Lorenzo was involved in at the time. A few years later John Paul II returned to Washington. When he met Lorenzo at St. Matthews he said: "Lorenzo, maybe now you will answer my letters."

Years later Lorenzo was called to Rome to present plans for the John Paul II Institute along with a father from Opus Dei. The priest from Opus Dei was impeccably dressed in his cassock; well-groomed for the occasion. He had his copious and well-developed notes in a beautiful leather binder. The priest began by saying: "Your Holiness, I did not sleep at all last night knowing that today I would have to make this presentation to the Vicar of Christ on Earth." He then made a very formal and thorough presentation of his well-developed ideas. Afterwards Pope John Paul turned to Lorenzo and asked him to make his presentation. Lorenzo, with a menu of two weeks on his clerical shirt, began by saying: "Your Holiness, Your Holiness, I slept very well last night." Lorenzo then produced an envelope from

Riggs Bank, from his suit coat pocket and declared: "I had an overdraft in my checking account, so the bank notified me and sent me this envelope." He then read his brilliant notes from the back of the envelope and thoroughly entertained St. Pope John Paul II.

We must be careful not to be so dazzled by Lorenzo's incredible sense of humor. Fue el hombre más occurente que había conocido en toda mi vida. (He was the most clever man I met in all of my life.) There was so much more to Lorenzo. What was so out there included: his zany wit, his unkempt appearance, his disorganized life, his financial problems, his phobias, and his eccentricities. But as Erasmus said of Thomas More: "He was made and born for friendship." What a capacity for unconditional love! He made everyone feel at home, and you knew that you were with a friend. "En el crepusculo de la vida, seremos juzgados solo por el amor," said San Juan de la Cruz. *"At the end of our life we will be judged only by how much we loved."*

Lorenzo's love for his family, for Conchita, for Manolo, and for friends on every continent, Catholics and atheists, Jews and Protestants, was unfailing. Lorenzo's love touched everybody, whether they were from Triumph Magazine or the New Republic. He had what the Spanish call "don de gente." (He was good with people.)

That capacity for love, compassion, and empathy, made Lorenzo a great friend and a great priest, because the goodness of the Good Shepherd could be glimpsed in his goodness. Lorenzo's was not an easy life and his problems were a great source of worry to those of

22

us who were close to him. There were so many false starts. Lorenzo's meteoric career as President of the Universidad Católica in Ponce. After Lorenzo lost his job as Rector, I sent him two quotes from Fray Luis de León:

Vida Retirada
"Que descansada vida
la del que huye del mundanal ruido
y sigue la escondida senda
por donde han ido
los pocos sabios que en el mundo han sido."[1]

After experiencing what envy and intrigue can do to you, Lorenzo was like Fray Luis who wrote:

Al Salir de la Cárcel
"Y con pobre mesa y casa
en el campo deleitoso
con solo Dios se compasa
y a solas su vida pasa
ni envidiado ni envidioso. " [2]

Lorenzo's tenure at Dunwoody was cut short; and his writing for the Sunday Magazine of New York Times came to naught.

---

1 Fray Luis de Leon, To Retirement, "What a rested life / the one that flees far from the maddening crowd / and follows the hidden / path where they have gone / the few wise people in the world have been!

2 Fray Luis de Leon, When Leaving Prison "and with a poor table and house,/ in the delightful field/ with God alone,/ alone his life goes by,/ neither envied nor envious. "

But all of the pain and disappointment was dissipated because of Lorenzo's friendship with Don Giussani. Communion and Liberation was a God send for Lorenzo. And I believe that Lorenzo was a God send for CL. God's loving providence engineered this wonderful match. Lorenzo loved young people and was such a gifted teacher and mentor to them. His genius was to be able to dialogue with the culture, science, and with the media. His intellect was so bright and still more illumined by his deep faith.

The love and devotion of the CL Community, Olivetta Danese, and so many who really cared for Lorenzo and allowed him to accomplish so much, to blossom. All of the wonderful articles in Tracce and other publications, and the retreats and conferences would never have happened without the help and support of CL. Lorenzo dedicated his book *God at the Ritz* to Don Giussani from whom Lorenzo learned so much. Lorenzo defines suffering as a thirst for meaning, for understanding, for solidarity, for friendship, for affirmation. Lorenzo said:

"The one who suffers wants to be assured that he or she is not crazy, guilty, or an outcast for life. I have tried to show how suffering can be a point of departure towards an encounter with Mercy as the origin and destiny of life."

Today we are consoled that Lorenzo's suffering was that point of departure, a preface to an encounter with Mercy. The Emmaus story documents the encounter of two disciples, overcome with grief and fear, and the Risen Christ who seeks them out like the Hound of Heaven. It is the story of a journey and an encounter, two concepts dear to Don Giussani and Lorenzo. It is the story of pain and loss, being transformed into new life and joy. The disciples are running from Calvary, they are seeking safety and they find Christ. Or Christ finds them. They engage in a conversation. *Cor ad cor loquitur.* (Heart speaking to heart.) Their hearts are burning within them. Lorenzo engaged in so many of those conversations that allowed people to discover the reality of Christ. Lorenzo's journey touched the lives of many fellow travelers and allowed them to experience Christ no longer as a stranger, but as a friend. In his own brokenness, Lorenzo could break open the word of God and release its power.

To me, one of the most fascinating lines in this Gospel is where Luke records that Jesus "gave the impression that He was going on farther." At that moment the disciples might have said: "Great talking to you. So long. See you around." This Gospel would never have been written if they had not invited Jesus to stay with them. Christ wants to be invited. At supper, Jesus shares with them His identity and allows them to recognize Him in His self-giving in the breaking of the bread. In St. Matthew's Cathedral the De Rosen mosaic behind the altar of the Blessed Sacrament depicts the two disciples filled with Eucharistic amazement and the inscription declares: "They recognized Him in the breaking of the bread." The Lord disappears, but the bread remains, now in the tabernacle, the Body and Blood of Christ.

They set out at once and returned to Jerusalem. They were now willing to risk their lives to share the Good News. They become participants of the mission of their Master to bring glad tidings, to liberate those captive by fear in the Cenacle, to place on those who mourn in Zion a diadem instead of ashes.

I like to think that Cleopas and his buddy were at the Cenacle with Mary and the Apostles for the outpouring of the Spirit on the Church. And I see them in today's second reading from Acts, part of that community, devoted to the teaching of the Apostles, holding all their material goods in common, caring for the needs of all, and most importantly gathering in their homes for the breaking of the bread. Discipleship really is about liberation and communion. And the joy of knowing that the Lord added to their numbers those who were being saved.

Lorenzo's journey was an Emmaus journey where Christ the stranger becomes Christ the friend and liberator. Lorenzo was an eloquent messenger of the joy of the Gospel. He found his strength in the Eucharist; he recognized Jesus in the breaking of the Bread.

Let me conclude with the prayer of an old priest, painfully aware of his own limitations and brokenness who reflects that when he lifts the host, he is overwhelmed by his own unworthiness, and he pleads with God that just as the priest held God in his unworthy hands, that God will never let him slip from God's divine hands.

PLEGARIA DE UN SACERDOTE
(by Lope de Vega)

Cuando en mis manos, Rey eterno, os miro
y la cándida víctima levanto,
de mi atrevida indignidad me espanto
y la piedad de vuestro pecho admiro.
Tal vez el alma con temor retiro,
tal vez la doy al amoroso llanto,
que, arrepentido de ofenderos tanto,
con ansias temo y con dolor suspiro.
Volved los ojos a mirarme humanos,
que por las sendas de mi error siniestras
me despeñaron pensamientos vanos;
no sean tantas las desdichas nuestras
que a quien os tuvo en sus indignas manos
vos le dejeis de las divinas vuestras.

PRAYER OF A PRIEST
(by Lope de Vega)

When in my hands, Eternal King, I look at you
and the innocent victim I raise,
of my daring indignity I am frightened
and the pity of your breast I admire.

Perhaps the soul with fear retires,
perhaps I give it to the loving cry,
that, repented of offenses so much,
with anxieties I fear and with pain I sigh.

Turn your eyes to look at me humans,
that by the sinister paths of my error
I was thrown into vain thoughts;

Our misfortunes are not so many
that to those who had you in their unworthy hands,
you leave them the divine ones.

Heavenly Father,
In thy hands we commend our brother, Lorenzo.
Hold on tight.

The Existence of God

Lecture
St. Catherine's Parish
Wheaton, MD, 1967

If you go to a place where paperback books are sold these days, you are bound to find out almost invariably that there are a number of books dealing with the unbelievable crimes committed against millions and millions of innocent people by the Nazis during the last World War. In a sense this is a good indication, because we most certainly need to be reminded of what we are capable of doing. And mind you, this was not done thousands of years ago during a "barbarian age," nor was it done by some uncivilized tribe in an obscure jungle. This was done in the very 20th century, within the lifetime of our own parents: this so-called century of progress, of science, of technology- and by a group of people in one of the most civilized countries of the world: "ordinary" people, educated people, people like our friends, our neighbors, the man across the street. Indeed, as someone wrote that the house of civilization proved to be no shelter.

But when all of this is acknowledged, it remains nevertheless true that there can be too much of it. Many of these books are evidently not written to remind us of what can happen if certain principles are ignored, but rather they are written to appeal to a weird mentality which seems to relish the details of these monstrous crimes, or to enjoy the confirmation that we can really be this evil.

Therefore, whenever I see one of these books, I am very hesitant in buying it, unless I am sure that it has something to contribute. This evening I would like to begin our discussion by quoting to you from one such book. The book is *Babi Yar*, by the Russian author, Anatoly Kuznetsov, and it deals with his experiences as a 12 year-old boy in a Soviet city occupied by the Nazis during the war.[1] One finds it hard even to imagine what to be alive meant to these captive people. It would be very hard for someone with a good imagination (if "good" is the correct adjective) to invent so much misery, so much degradation, so much injustice. And all seemingly for nothing! These victims had done absolutely nothing to deserve this fate, except, it appears, to have been born. You may begin to imagine what this was like when you are accused of doing that which you know you simply have not done. It is this feeling, so hard to describe, which leads this 12 year-old boy to raise his voice to heaven and to speak with words which should give pause to any man of conscience. Listen to what he says:

---

1 Kuznetsov, Anatoly; Babi Yar; New York; Farrar, Straus and Giroux; 1970

"All this without having been a member of the Communist Party, the Young Communist League, or the underground. Nor was I a Jew, a gypsy, or a hostage.

I had not made any speeches or owned pigeons or a radio. I was just a most ordinary, average, nondescript little fellow in a cap! But by their rule, whatever you do, you'll be punished – I already did not have the right to live..."

"But I want to live!"
"I want to live as long as I was meant to, and not as long as you degenerate bipeds decide I should."
"How dare you?"
"What right have you to decide my life, to decide:
How long I shall live,
How I shall live,
Where I shall live,
What I shall think,
What I shall feel
And when I shall die?"

I ask you now to consider this child's plea. Do you think he is right?
Do you think his complaint is fair?
Do you agree with what he asks?
Why?

Why do you think this way? Not why should it be this way, but why do you, whatever your name is, why do you think this boy is right? What is it in you that decides what is fair and what is unfair, what is just and what is unjust? This is not a stupid question. For when you look at it, we have here a 12 year-old boy accusing a world of injustice. An "ordinary, nondescript, little fellow in a cap" standing against people much older than him, supposedly more wise, a boy standing in the way of a major world power, of international diplomacy – in the way of the forces of history and saying, "This is wrong!"

Turn the question around. As him – and yourselves as well: "Why not? Why should you be the one to decide? How dare you question an army, a government, a nation. Who do you think you are?"
And yet...you know it, in your souls, you know it... this boy is right.
Why?
Think about it.

I have been asked to speak to you tonight about the existence of God. But let me tell you: tonight, I want you to think about questions like these. If you do not, then what I will say will mean nothing at all.

But I think that you will. We are told that these types of questions are bothering the youth of today. They are said to "feel" things better – they are "with it," they know the "scene," they have "the thing;" they "tell it like it is."

Well, this is like it is! I speak to you tonight of God. Not of God as the origin of the stars and the galaxies, or as the just cause in an endless chain of causes, although He is, of course, all of this. Not of a God who is somewhere "out there" watching over you, waiting to trap you. I wish to proclaim to you tonight the God who is within you – the God of the scene – yes, the God of the thing.

And so, we return to our first question. Why do we think as we do? What tells us what is just and fair? What on earth leads us to believe that one single human being has inalienable rights – that we cannot treat people like animals as just one more social security number – that there is such a thing as dignity, justice, and rights. What do these words mean anyway?

Does the earth have dignity?

Must you be just with the wind?

Do the stars have rights? Does a man?

Why?

The earth, the wind, and the stars are much more powerful than man, certainly more majestic. Why man, then?

An African poet, John Okai, protesting against a colonialism which seeks to impose a foreign way of life upon his people, recently wrote:

> *"Just as I am*
> *Just as I am--*
> *Counted with those who breathe,*
> *You cannot break my bone,*
> *Just as you can*
> *Not scan the sun...*
> *You cannot shake my spear*
> *Just as you can*
> *Not count the stars...*
> *You cannot grade my grain*
> *Just as you can*

Not catch the wind.
So let fighting flies fight,
And leave my land to me!"

And so, again, we ask, "How come?" Why is he more than the sun, the stars, and the wind?

Why? Once more: why do we think this way?

Some would tell us that it is because we have been trained this way from childhood. Men have learned that it is necessary to respect the other person's rights because otherwise we would have disorder, and chaos. And so, they teach this to their children, they pass it on, and we all grow up with this sense of justice. It is simply self-preservation.

Now, part of this argument is true. Certainly, our background, our education has a lot to do with our feelings of right and wrong. But as we grow up, we learn (at least, we should learn) to question what we have been taught, and when we do this, we should be able to judge, as it were, our own consciences. So then: suppose that in a given situation the recognition of a people's rights would lead to disorder. Suppose that it were to become necessary for the preservation of "order" or "stability" to kill innocent people. Would you say it would then be right?

I would hope not. There is still something within us which rejects this solution regardless of the consequences. Something that still tells us that human life is sacred.

Again, why? The existence of God! It is not an easy subject... especially these days when so much is changing it is necessary to think about these things. Perhaps it will be that because so much is changing, we will find something which will help us get along.

Open almost any old book on religion, and you will find in it "proofs" of the existence of God. I do not wish to pass judgment on these. But tonight, it seems to me, it would be hard, very hard, to produce a positive, direct, universally valid and so-called scientifically objective proof of the existence of God. It would seem to require knowledge in so many separate areas, an ability to master complicated and difficult methods.

Not that I am unaware of scientific proofs. I am, by profession, a scientist. But in science, I have learned of the existence of mystery. And tonight, I wish you to taste a mystery which is beyond us: to taste, to experience, to feel, to let it happen — we have learned these words from you — they are your vocabulary.

You have already seen that there are certain questions which we cannot answer without coming into contact with something more than ourselves, something beyond us. A German theologian, Karl Rahner, wrote about this experience in an article in his book, *Belief Today*.[2] One of his points is this: you can think of God especially when you are aware in your life of certain times when you come into contact with what we may call "the spirit." Note, this "spirit" is not some gooey, scary thing—not some sentimental feeling—but actually something within you and at the same time beyond you.

---

2 Rahner, Kar; Belief Today, New York, Sheed & Ward, First Edition, 1967

In these instances, you experience what theologians call the "transcendent." Consider some of the examples he gives:

1. Can you remember one occasion when you kept silent although you longed to defend yourself and although you were in danger of being unjustly dealt with?
2. Did you ever freely forgive someone from whom you expected nothing in return and who would take your silent forgiveness simply as a matter of course?
3. Did you ever make a sacrifice that was unnoticed, thankless, and did not even give you a sense of inner satisfaction?
4. Were you ever really, utterly alone?
5. Did you ever decide on something following your own conscience, something that could not be discussed with or explained to anybody else, knowing anyway that it was your responsibility and that you had to answer first?
6. Have you ever tried to persevere in the love of someone even when all emotion and enthusiasm had deserted you – when it seemed that such love would be the death of you – when all you could see in it was the renunciation of everything: life, as well as all else?
7. Have you ever said "yes, there is meaning to life," even when everything seemed to be incomprehensible, empty?

8. Have you ever done a kindness to someone because you knew you had to, even if this involved something apparently stupid and thankless?

Think about experiences like these in your life. If such an experience ever came your way, then you have had a brief encounter with eternity — you have tasted the spirit – you have known that the significance of life is not of the same kind as the significance of this world, or worldly happiness—that certain dangers can be faced with a confidence completely unconnected with worldly results.

Perhaps it appears that we are going around in circles. But as I have said, we are not tonight after a neat, logical outline of a clear, fool-proof argument for the existence of God. Instead I want you to begin to think about the way you are, the way you look at things, the way you answer questions like these. To be able to do this you must be very honest with yourselves.

You must enter into the very heart of yourselves, where there are no more excuses and no more deceptions. I ask you to begin a trip into your inner world. We hear a lot these days about trips. But ours tonight must be a serious inquiry, not like many of the "experiences" that are popular with some; experiences imposed by external agents, such as drugs. These experiences in the final analysis depend on artificial stimulants and are therefore not really sincere. After all, you can strike someone, and he will feel pain. This is perfectly natural. Stop doing it, and the pain will cease. What we have in mind tonight is not something that depends on a self-induced feeling – but rather, a very honest analysis of ourselves as we are – we want to discover why we are this way, why we think things are fair, right, just – why is it that there are moments when we experience a mystery beyond words, a great, unanswered question. These experiences are by no means ordinary, nor are they easily arrived at. It is so easy to deceive ourselves! It is so easy to confuse emotion with wisdom; moodiness with revelation! Our experience of the spirit must survive the test of reality. Long after the exhilaration is gone, when we are alone with the hard facts of life which must be faced; what we have learned, what we have seen, must endure these trials.

This is a trip not after certainty, but after understanding. But not understanding in the abstract, but understanding of ourselves.

Many of you perhaps saw the film, *A Man for all Seasons*.[3] It is, as you know the story of a man who would not betray himself by swearing to what he considered false and who lost his life as a result of his refusal to take an oath. We need not be concerned here about the substance of the oath nor as to what it was that he rejected in it. Nor do we have to concern ourselves with the question of whether signing an oath is that important, nor with whether there could have been a way out. What interests us here is the fact that there comes a time for a man when he feels that he cannot compromise further, that he cannot "go along"

---

3 Zinnemann, Fred, dir.; A Man for All Seasons; 1966; Los Angeles, CA; Columbia Pictures, 120 min.

anymore, for by doing so he would be betraying himself. That is to say, certain issues, certain questions, go to the very heart of what we are, or better still – who we think we are. And at that point we discover that we cannot go against our own opinion of ourselves, against our values, our judgments. We can go along most of the time, we can compromise, even if we are sorry later – all of this is possible – but there comes that time in which we feel we have reached the limit, and to go on further would be a betrayal of our own self. Many of us of course, most of us really, have not experienced this – and indeed possibly never will. But I think we can imagine what it means. We have seen others who stand up for what they believe – whatever consequence may follow. Naturally, it is again very easy to deceive ourselves, to confuse stubbornness with honesty. Many indeed solemnly proclaim that this or that would be against their consciences when the truth is that they have substituted their desires for their consciences. And yet, because the fact that appeals to conscience have been misused, it does not imply that they are per se invalid. We have in *A Man for All Seasons* the example of St. Thomas More.

Robert Bolt, the author of the play, (who by the way does not consider himself a Christian, not even a believer) states in his introduction:

"A man takes an oath only when he wants to commit himself entirely to the statement, when he wants to

make an identity between the truth of it and his own virtue – he offers his own self as a guarantee."[4]

That is, we feel that the self is sacred, that we cannot give it away easily; that we cannot commit it indiscriminately. There is something within us which we regard as invulnerable. Consider the words of More himself:

"What matters to me is not whether it is true or not, but that I believe it to be true—or rather not that I believe it, but that I believe it."[5]

To me it has to be (this way), for that's myself. Affection goes as deep in me as you think, but only God is love right through, and that's myself.

When a man takes an oath, he is holding his own self in his own hands, like water. And if he opens his fingers then he needn't hope to find himself again. Finally, it isn't a matter of reason--finally, it is a matter of me.

And so again we come to the same question. Does a man feel this way? What is this self that is so sacred?

If there exists nothing beyond ourselves, no final mystery to which we must be faithful, then why?

There does seem to be this mystery, and once more we meet it. In asking questions like this, we are entering

---

4 Bolt, Robert; A Man for all Seasons: A Play in Two Acts; London; Samuel French; 1960

5 Bolt, Robert; A Man for all Seasons: A Play in Two Acts; London; Samuel French; 1960; pp 49 (emphasis original). It should be noted that this is not a quote from the historical Thomas More, but reflects the views of Bolt.

its world. When we experience this mystery, we are detecting the limits of human intelligence, and we seem to stand speechlessly before the transcendent.

Many of you are perhaps familiar with the scientific (or mathematical) concept of the field, such as the electric field. We have, for example, two electric charges and they exert forces on one another: no charges, no forces. Many times, in electricity we are interested in obtaining the force on one charge due to all the other charges present. Now, it is possible to calculate this by a formula which takes into account every "other" charge. However, this can get pretty messy, especially if there are many charges present, or even more if we do not even know exactly where they are. What we do then is to imagine that all the charges present create a field, sort of like a "space filled with force" which depends indeed on the present charges, but which can be calculated, added, subtracted, etc., without considering the particular charges themselves. In fact, after a while we forget about the charges that cause this force field and just imagine that it is a characteristic of the space itself — every point in it feels a certain force which depends on where that point is. It is something like the wind, it is blowing all over, caused indeed by something, but we do not care- all we know is that the minute we put something in it, it will feel a force, it will be blown in a certain definite direction, a direction and a force which is characteristic of the type of "wind field" it is.

The reason I bring up all of this, is that I think that it is possible to speak of a "value field," a "judgment field" or a "way of being field" associated with every person. Our own field determines how we look at things, what we consider good or bad, beautiful or ugly, just or unjust. In a sense we can say that each one of us is a value field. The moment something or someone comes to our awareness, it "feels" the effect of our field, that is, it will be judged or valued by us. We will say, not immediately perhaps, but often using the characteristics of our field, (applying our "field equations" as it were) we will say: "I agree, I disagree, I like you, it is wrong, it is fair, etc."

You always have an opinion of everything you are aware of, even if it is the opinion that you have no opinion.

Tonight, you must begin to ask yourself: what is your field like? How do you think of yourself; by what standards do you judge other people, all events? What do you hope for and why do you hope at all? Why do you look for the meaning of things, why do you want to understand? Why do you think some things are more meaningful than others? What is your world view, what is your life policy? What leads you to what you are? What is the main point of your understanding and your living? Finally, how do you experience yourself as a person different from the others? Have you ever been aware of being yourself and nobody else?

In trying to answer these questions, I believe, you will come into contact with the mystery of existence. You cannot, of course, answer all of these questions at once, in one night. In fact, perhaps you can never answer them entirely. But if you think about them now, and later at home, you will see that they are indeed valid and important questions. Questions that indeed exist, and to say that they do not is already in a way to declare that they do, for otherwise you would not have bothered about them.

Everyone has a field, everyone has a reason for living, everyone has reasons for doing as they do, for hoping as they hope, and for judging as they judge. To say that things have no meaning is contradicting because such a statement is in itself more meaningful to you than to say that there is meaning — just like the man who says "there is not law" without realizing that that is as much a law as any other.

So, you see, this mystery is inescapable, it is always present, we cannot hide from it. It is, in fact, almost a field itself. A field which judges us, which is present in all that we do or think. We are silent before it, because we know it is greater than us. And yet, it is an attractive field. The force which we feel when we become aware of this field is a force of attraction: it is a call which leads us on and on without ever exhausting itself. But we are not objects, we are persons. Therefore, the call of this field is a call to a person — for only two persons can ever truly call each other. Hence this mystery, this mysterious field which we had glimpsed in all of these questions tonight now appears to be a Personal field, a Personal Mystery. We do not know its name. We only know it is not anybody else we know.

We call him God—the One who is, the one who calls. Now at last we have arrived. Now at last we may speak the name. Silently. He was edging us on. Now, for an instant, we know His name. We have seen the invisible, and nothing will ever be the same again.

Of course, we have said nothing about what this mystery is like in itself; its Personal life, its power, its way of knowing. Let all of this come later, some other time. For tonight, we are content in knowing the name. And once we do, the quest is endless, the treasures limitless. St. Paul says: "The length, the width, the height and the depth." [6]

To understand it we must begin to taste it, to acquire the habit of thinking this way about ourselves, about our values, and about our actions. Then we will begin to glimpse the eternal, the transcendent, the world of God.

There is so much noise these days! We must look for a moment of silence, so that we may hear this voice calling in the wilderness. We must learn again to meditate. Indeed, we hear that this is becoming increasingly popular among the young today. Some are even going to India in search of meditation. But there is no need to go that far. We may learn to do it here, in our hearts. Then we may discover that there is always one with us whom we many times do not dare name.

One of the Beatles recently said, "The four of us have had the most hectic lives. We have got almost anything that money can buy. But when you can do

---

6 Ephesians 3:14-21

that, the things you buy mean nothing. After a time, you look for something else, for a new experience." [7] It is this experience which we have encountered tonight. We have seen that there are times in the life of a man when he is aware of a mystery at the very heart of his person, a mystery which lets itself be analyzed, but which in the end is always beyond us. It is a sort of unrest, a desire to understand. A mystery which is at the same time seen and unseen. It "speaks in its silence" and is "present in its absence." We call this God.

He is the source of both the unrest and the rest of my spirit, the one who prompts my desire to understand and fulfills it. This drive that leads me to give attention, to make sense of things, even to challenge and to judge myself is of God and nothing else will give it rest but He alone. He is before the beginning of every question and He remains after every answer. Words are not enough to describe Him, and our concepts cannot trap Him entirely. He always slips away. Nevertheless, we ask.

We look at ourselves, and He is there. We look at our history, and He gives it sense. Even little things acquire unutterable depths. The person we love appears as a messenger of eternity. In the words of the song:

"The words of the Prophets are written on the subway walls, tenement halls—and whispered in the sound of silence." [8]

---

7 Coleman, John E.; The Quiet Mind; Pariyatti Publishing; USA; Quote from Ringo Starr, p.140

8 Simon & Garfunkel; Wednesday Morning, 3 A.M.; The Sound of Silence, Columbia Records; 1964

If a joke has a point, if a problem has a solution, if things have any meaning, it is because men can understand, and jokes, problems, and things are understandable. The source of this understanding in man is in part, what we mean by God. In naming God, therefore, we intend to name the one who responds to the why at the center of my questioning. He is not one explanation, but He is the explanation of why there are explanations. Finally, the man who has tasted God knows that life is not static, that it is a response to a call. To know is not enough. The world today is in need of men of action. We would do well to remember the words of St. Paul:

"If I have the eloquence of men or of angels,
but speak without love,
I am simply a gong booming
or a cymbal clashing.
If I have the gift of prophecy,
understanding all the mysteries there are,
and knowing everything,
and if I have faith in all its fullness,
to move mountains,
but without love, then I am nothing at all."[9]

My friends: we have not even begun tonight to scratch the surface of this great mystery. Someone said:

"If I should take my stand
on the shore of your Endlessness,
And shout into the trackless reaches
of your being all the words

---

9 Corinthians 13:4-7

I have learned in the poor prison
of my little existence,
what should I have said?
I should never have spoken
the last word about you. " [10]

We are also Christians. As such we dare to proclaim that there is One in whom this mystery has been revealed. We cannot end tonight without speaking His name: the Lord Jesus.

"He is the radiant light of God's glory,
and the perfect copy of His nature,
sustaining the universe
by His powerful command." [11]

We are left in the end with our own hours of silence, our own lonely confrontations with the darkness in which God may or may not lie hidden. Conversation with friends, the reading of books, a talk like tonight's: these may help. But in the end each man is alone in the silence. In that moment, words, images, concepts, and representations of all sorts fade away. And at that time we will have to decide. Prepare yourselves now. Some will say that we are being deceived. I do not think so.

For me, at any rate, it has been said from the beginning:

"Lord, to whom else shall we go?" [12]

Thank you.

---

10 Rahner, Karl; Encounters with Silence; South Bend, IN; St. Augustine's Press; 1999; p. 4
11 Hebrews 1:3
12 John 6:68

Christianity According to Monsignor

A Letter to His Godson
April 28, 1968

Dear Michael John:

A few days after your birth, my brother and I went to Holy Cross to bid you welcome, for our part, into this land of men, into this society, into this world. After a short time spent congratulating the producers and agents responsible for your appearance, live and in color, on this planet, we were ushered into your most august presence.

I must say that you appeared quite unimpressed with your new surroundings and your assembled fan club, preferring to devote your attention to those around you, also arrived from that land we have all possibly forgotten, but which you and your friends apparently still vividly remembered. You look relieved that at least someone had been sensible enough to erect a glass wall protecting you from the adulation of your admirers. Now I have been charged, much more officially, to

49

welcome you into another land: a new society, a new world. It is a much more difficult task, as you will realize by the time you understand this letter.

I imagine your parents knew what they were doing when they asked me to perform this task. For you see, I have been exposing them to my version of this world long before your appearance. The settings for my discourses ranged from a conference room in an old Marine barracks (now with the more formal but no less inspiring name of "Building 90"), to a scattering of Hot Shoppes restaurants (were my essays were inspired by large doses of banana splits), from a Middle Eastern ship in the Baltimore harbor (!!), to an impossibly confined space, wrapped in a super structure which your father insisted on dignifying with the name "car." It should not surprise you then that my first message to you is in the form of this crazy letter. I promise to expound on my views whenever you request it, but I will never impose these on you, which is the least I can do in view of the fact that you were never consulted concerning my selection. More than this, whatever I have said today in your name, I have said with the understanding that you will in the future either ratify or reject it, after examining the evidence.

For evidence there indeed is, only that it is not easy to distinguish, it takes so long at times, Michael, to begin to understand the laws of life in this other world, to breathe its air, and to see its signs. Today you have, as it were, been given new eyes, new ears, new hands, a new tongue, and even a new nose. Now you must learn to use them. To see, to hear, to touch, to smell, and to talk about this new life which is infused throughout the other: like the sea water which wets the shore and goes temporarily away, like the breeze which moves the leaves on the trees in Rock Creek park.

If you do not use these new senses, they will atrophy, they will surely die. If this happens, you will see nothing, you will not hear the sounds of life, you will detect no sweet fragrance, you will extend your hands and touch no one. Your talk will be in vain.

But if you do develop your new senses, you will come into contact with life (after perhaps a painful and bitter struggle, but a pain that becomes joy, and struggle that leads to victory and peace). If you do read the signs of Its presence amongst men, then your eyes will see beauty, you will hear music, your touch will be soft, you will grasp at times an incomparable fragrance, and your talk will be wisdom.

If you fail (forgive me for being blunt), then all that fuss at Holy Cross will have been in vain.

But you will not fail. You have been given a good home, blessed parents, and at least for my part, a friend. If you live up to these gifts, and up to the memory of those who have gone before you (and I must think here of your grandfather, to whom, I must say, I sneaked a little bit of my doctrine. Yes, he too did not escape, although I hate to admit that now he has surpassed us all). If you assimilate these things, and give them your own touch, your own free commitment (for each man must be himself), then you will win the battle, you will have fought the good fight, you will have won the race. With your new senses, you will have felt the invisible.

Suddenly, everything is converted into its opposite. Darkness into light, enslavement into freedom, death into life, taking into giving, destruction into creation, and hate into love.

Welcome, then, into this strange land: where the cripple walk, the deaf hear, the mute speak, the blind see, and even the mountains move!

Begin, then, to read the signs of its presence in the lives around you and in the lives of history; in the teachings of your Church, and in the example of your parents. But above all, in the life, in the teachings, in the example of the One whose coming makes us infinitely proud of this poor planet which welcomed you earlier: The Lord Jesus.

There is another glass wall, like the one at Holy Cross, which separates man from this new life. He has shown us how it can be broken.

As your godfather, society expects me to give you, now and then, "presents." I do not really have much to give, Michael, at least from society's viewpoint. But I pledge to you now that I will do all I can to help you destroy that wall, and enter into the new life, and, in the end, the new world.

Sincerely,
Uncle Lolo

Engineered Divinity

Book Review of:
The Immortalist
by Alan Harrington
New York City; Random House; 1969

Triumph Magazine, September 1969, pp. 32-34

Rene Descartes did not want to die. And so he set out
to do something about it. Supremely confident of his
"method," he undertook a quest for a "mathematically
demonstrated medicine" which would abolish death
— only the search took longer than he expected.
As recounted by Etienne Gilson (in The Unity of
Philosophical Experience), by 1646 (four years
before his death), Descartes had turned his attention
to ethics, and a "method" which taught him not
to fear death. "A very useful discovery," remarks
Gilson, "but a rather old one, and one which does
not require the brains of a physico-mathematician."

Mr. Alan Harrington does not like dying either. So he
has decided to consider the alternative: to eliminate

death. How and why this is to be accomplished is the subject of Mr. Harrington's new book *The Immortalist*.

First of all, how. How else? Through science, through technology, through the "Engineering of Man's Divinity" (as the book's subtitle has it). But can science in fact abolish death, and if so, how? To ask this question is cultural blasphemy. After all, we have landed a man on the moon, and yes, we did crack the atom. Moreover, there is the State of the Biomedical Arts.

"Blood Cells May Be Crown in Laboratory," "Debakey Sees Brain Transfers," "Barnard Predicts Animal Heart Use," "Pa. Doctors Study…" "Physicians Say… "Dr. Cooley Planning…" and so on, and so on, and so on. "May be," "sees," "predicts," "study," "say," "planning." …So much for the State of the Biomedical Arts in this book.

"A new act of faith is required of us," writes Mr. Harrington, "a belief that with the technology we will soon have at our disposal, death can eventually be conquered. This faith must accept as gospel that salvation belongs to medical engineering…"

So much for Mr. Harrington's science.

The problem, however, is not Mr. Harrington's science, as science. The problem is that after the Mr. Harringtons get through enough television shows their "science" will appear as science. Mr. Harrington's "science" is not new. What is new are the vast powers of respectability available to this type of "science."

As Fr. Stanley Jaki, OSB writes in *The Relevance of Physics*:

> *"Epigones whose number and vociferousness*
> *always outweigh the wise counsel of masters*
> *lose no time in presenting hypotheses*
> *as demonstrated verities."*

The masters have always insisted that true scientific predictions about the future must be based on what is actually known, and not on an evasion of enormous problems. There is no authority, scientific or otherwise, that can predict with any reliability the shape of discoveries to come. As long as science remains what it is supposed to be, a discourse about experimental data and experimentally verifiable statements, sheer conjectures should never be vested with the aura of scientific respectability. Speculations on what the future may or may not bring cannot transform a mere possibility into a fact. This is why the path of "scientific predictions" is quite precarious, and why the history of science abounds with most embarrassing examples. Mr. Harrington's "science," as he admits himself, is nothing but faith, and a scientific faith is as susceptible to obscurantism as any.

How far biological engineering can go, no one knows, nor in any "scientific" way can predict. How far it ought to go, however, is another question. Both the Christian and the biological engineer agree that man is over nature. But the Christian knows that man and nature are under God. The question is: are man's birth and death a part of the nature that man is over, or a part of the man that God is over? The Catholic answer is unequivocal: "Every problem regarding human life is to be considered, beyond partial perspectives – whether of the biological or psychological, demographic, or sociological orders – in the light of an integral vision of man and of his vocation, not only his material and earthly, but also his supernatural and eternal vocation" (*Humanae Vitae*). Moreover: "The Church is the first to praise and recommend the intervention of intelligence in a function which so closely associates the rational creature with his creator (and death, like birth, is certainly in this category), but she affirms that this must be done with respect for the order established by God."

The purpose of human life is eternal union with God. It is in this light that men must view the question of death. Death is not something which happens to a man accidentally. It is the moment in which the very man himself becomes his definitive self. It is the moment in which, transcending space and time, his eternal destiny is realized, and his reason for being fulfilled. And so even if biological death might be postponed or overcome by science, man's separation from God, and thus his radical insufficiency, cannot be abolished by medical engineering. There always must be true death.

The Immoralist's view of death is entirely simplistic; death is not a mere biological misfortune. It is a question, first of all, of man's destiny, and then, of sin.

The destiny of the human spirit is only partially fulfilled in this world, regardless of how long a man might live.

So much is this so that some assert that even without sin, man would have ended his biological, and historical life in space and time, and would have entered into his definitive condition before God by means of a free act engaging his whole life, that is, by some sort of "death."

The New Testament (Cor 15:51) recognizes that even after sin, those who will be found alive at Christ's second coming must attain eternal life by a radical change which in substance is the same as death. The consequence of sin is to make this experience obscure. Ambiguous, painful, that is, what we commonly understand as death. Death is not simply an arbitrary punishment, but is intrinsically connected with separation from God. Death is a consequence of sin, and no amount of scientific discoveries can alter this fact: science cannot free man from sin.

Remarkably, Mr. Harrington's book gives ample testimony to the sinful condition of man. It is his intention to ground the "Immortalist point of view" on the "evidence that since the beginning of recorded time man has engaged in a disguised drive to make himself immortal and divine."

Mr. Harrington's survey of this drive is largely a fantastic display of name dropping. Moreover, we shall kindly dismiss much of his language as a desire to shock. Nevertheless, it is true that since the fall man has been "groaning" (remember St. Paul?) for union with God, and for salvation. Much of Mr. Harrington's history can be accepted by a Catholic as a devastating expose of man's attempt to evade this fundamental issue, especially today. Mr. Harrington admits as much: "Our source is Roman Catholic," he writes. His conclusion is not Roman Catholic because he has mistaken this urge as the desire to eliminate biological death when, in fact, man's frustration is rooted in his not being able to be fully human in the sense of being called to encounter God and to love Him wholeheartedly. The frustration is that of not being able to live the human life expected of an adopted human son of God.

This frustration, this tension, this discrepancy, this contradiction, is the death which is the result of sin. A natural biological death is the decisive moment in which this process is brought to its conclusion and resolved for all eternity. Furthermore, the true doctrine of immortality is grounded in reason as well as revelation. It cannot be obviated simply by saying that it isn't so. The fact that books of this kind can get away with just dismissing complex and profound issues which have occupied the human mind throughout history, and yet appear to be logical and "scientific" in the public mind is a sad comment on the state of the public mind.

The reader may decide for himself whether the immoralist utopia which Mr. Harrington describes is the type of human life he longs for. But to a generation convinced of the desirability of never-ending youth and change; to a people indoctrinated with the belief that man can create the heavenly city through social arrangements, this type of vision accords with the contemporary anxiety to keep people from dying rather than come to terms with death.

Before we rush headlong into a future filled with Swift's struldbruggs (and this is perhaps one of the minor evils that face us in a misguided technological era), let this question be engraved in the public mind: how long will God have patience with our evasion of His mercy in death and His love in life?

And so, Mr. Harrington, like Descartes, emerges as a man of faith. Their faiths are similar: each is a faith in man alone. Each attempts to evade the one Faith which alone can truly conquer death. "I am the resurrection and the life. If anyone believes in me, even though he dies, he will live; and whoever lives and believes in me SHALL NEVER DIE."

This artwork appeared with the book review
without an artist credit.

De-Schooling Illich

Book Review of: Deschooling Society
by Ivan Illich
Manhattan; Harper & Row; 1971

Triumph Magazine, November 1971, pp. 32-34

The thesis is stated simply in the second sentence of the Introduction: "We have come to realize that for most men the right to learn is curtailed by the obligation to attend school." Therefore, "The ethos, not just the institutions, of society ought to be 'de-schooled.'"

How, then, will "the right to learn'" be honored?

"The current search for new educational funnels must be reversed into the search for their institutional inverse: educational webs which heighten the opportunity for each one to transform each moment of his living into one of learning, sharing, and caring."

That, on one level, is the substance of Ivan Illich's argument. (A reading of Pius XI's *Divini Illius Magistri* 1929, would have led to more or less the same conclusions, of course. Still, one is happy that Ivan Illich has said it, for in the circles where he is popular, almost by definition, *Divini Illius Magistri* is not.) He is brilliant at describing the present totalitarianism of the School. Its fundamental sin is to have turned education into a commodity, subject to the same manipulation evident in other technocratic networks, for example in the so-called "transportation" system: "Highways result from a perversion of the desire and need for mobility into the demand for a private car. Schools themselves pervert the natural inclination to grow and learn into the demand for instruction."

The school, in fact, has been more successful than any other industry in creating consumer demand for its product, and is consequently so powerful that "work, leisure, politics, city living, and even family life depend on schools for the habits and knowledge they presuppose."

The principal victims of the corruption of education are the poor. In fact, their "poverty" itself is defined by their inability to purchase the commodity the schools distribute. The process is simple: education, a basic need, is transformed into a scientifically produced commodity, school instruction. Education is thus quantified, and technocrats are then free to set numerical standards that will measure a man's educational development. "Poverty then refers to those who have fallen behind an advertised ideal of consumption in some important respect." In education the "poverty level" is usually 12 years in school.

The standard is illegitimate; of course, because it substitutes process for substance. Yet the school system is the embodiment of this gnostic society's identity and faith; passage – processing – through it is the untouchable condition for social acceptance and growth. The school is "simultaneously the repository of society's myth, the institutionalization of the myth's contradictions, and the locus of the ritual which reproduces and veils the disparities between myth and reality."

But Ivan Illich is not interested only in analysis. Like any good physician, he makes a diagnosis only in order to discover a cure: "Only if school is understood as an industry can revolutionary strategy be planned realistically." The Christian will agree, since with respect to a society that has set up gods other than the Father of Our Lord Jesus Christ, he is at least at heart, a revolutionary. But the Christian will have to plan his own educational strategy, for Illich, it is painfully clear, is still trapped within the confines of the dialectic which made possible the existence of the oppressive school system in the first place. He attacks the schools for taking over the role of the Church in modern society, but not because he sees the take-over as a usurpation: he believes the role the Church formerly played in education should not be played at all, by anyone. That is, Illich's problem is with education itself: his book betrays a crippling confusion about what education is, who is its proper subject, and who its guardian.

The key to Illich's error is his analogy between the process called de-schooling and the process called secularization of Christian faith. "Since Bonhoeffer," he says "contemporary theologians have pointed to the confusions now reigning between the Biblical message and institutionalized religion. They point to the experience that Christian freedom and faith gain from secularization."

Well, in the first place, this experience is simply non-existent. Precisely the opposite is true of the most "de-schooled" of contemporary students, regardless of what theologians, who have been singularly blind these many years, may say. But more importantly, the fact is that the present imperialism of the schools would not have been possible without the process of secularization, which has denied the human spirit its proper food and left it to the school to pass out to its consumers artificial packages that do not nourish the starving society. Thus the monopoly of the schools can cease only when the student is given the opportunity to taste a true meal of the spirit – and it is the purpose of education to enable him to do just that. Would Illich's "educational webs" offer that opportunity? Not until Ivan Illich is himself de-schooled.

The process will require, first, that he understand properly the nature of the school's violation of education. A reading of *Divini Illius Magistri* might help. "School," wrote Pius XI, "considered in its historical origins, is by its very nature a subsidiary and complementary institution to the family and the Church; and the logical consequence of this fact is not only that the public school must not be contrary to the family and the Church, but also that it must be positively harmonized with these, in such a way that these three environments – school, family, Church – will constitute the one sanctuary of Christian education, lest the school be perverted and transformed into a pernicious influence on youth." What has broken the harmony among school, family, and Church? It is precisely the process of secularization which Illich hails.

In the public schools, secularization travels under the name of "neutrality" with respect to religion. Ironically, such "neutrality," to the degree that it truly exists, becomes an ideology, a religion of its own – that is, no neutrality at all! As Patrick Cardinal O'Boyle insisted recently in a Washington address, "Such neutrality is impossible in the education of children, who have not already formed a complete and self-conscious view of the world and of their own place in it." What is more, the institutionalization of this false neutrality stands in the way of the child forming such a "complete and self-conscious view," that is, of being educated.

An analogous phenomenon has taken place in the Catholic schools. Note that the key to a Christian education as defined by the pope is harmonizing positively the three environments into one sanctuary. No such sanctuary exists (if it ever did) today. The three environments of which the pope spoke are almost entirely isolated from one another. And the dissent from the magisterium of the Church that exists in many Catholic schools, however much it may contribute to the disruption of the family-school-Church bond, is not its fundamental cause. The real problem is that the organic unity which the Christian life demands as a condition for the education of its children has been broken by the surrender of the family and the school to the secularizing pressures of the dominant culture. The bond, where it exists at all, has become functional, a matter merely of convenience without the profundity which the word harmony implies. But functionalization, as Ivan Illich tells us, is the first step to quantification, the opening wedge for the packagers, the "professionals" who have wrapped education in plastic like any other commodity to be sold and consumed. Thus the importance of John Cardinal Wright's words to the Catechetical Congress meeting in Rome in September: "Even here, however, not so much 'professionals' are needed to teach the Faith; the great need is for committed, ardent, credible believers – not mere scientists, not mere 'technicians' – who, in one way or another, have seen the Lord Jesus, have had their lives transformed by His power, and, therefore, advance as their reason for being heard, not their academic degrees, their certificates or their accreditation, but the title that the Apostles claimed for themselves: 'We cannot do other than speak of those things that we have seen and heard' (Acts 4, 20)." Of late a new race has "taken the place of preachers, catechists, heralds of the Word, apostles of the Son of God, ambassadors of the Absolute: the strictly contemporary little group who call themselves 'professional theologians,' as others are professional bone setters, professional political theorists, professional tax experts, professional investment consultants, or professional therapists."

The appearance of the same phenomenon – "qualification by professionals" – in both religious and secular education, in both public and private schools, thus substantiates the conclusion that the problem is not precisely an "institutionalization of values," as Illich asserts, but the institutionalization of secularization as a value.

Secularization, neutrality, call it what you will: this is the culprit behind the phenomenon which Illich rightly decries – the quantification of education which makes possible the totalitarianism of the schools and which he mistakenly calls the institutionalization of value, instead of what it truly is, the institutionalization of no-value. Strike at this monster and you will really have a revolution. Illich is thus in the unenviable position of both fighting and encouraging the monster. Talk about the need for a liberating experience!

Ivan Illich's alternative to the schools may now be judged. He proposes the establishment of "no more than four – possibly even three – distinct 'channels' of learning exchanges." These "educational webs," which should contain all the resources needed for a real education, are: reference services to educational objects, skill exchanges, peer-matching and reference services to educators at large. "Things, models, peers and elders are four resources each of which requires a different type of arrangement to ensure that everybody has ample access to it."

The idea has its merits. It emphasizes contacts instead of programs, personal relationships instead of packages. But it will not resolve the educational impasse of modern society. Only if the webs become organic bonds will they do that; and they will not be this if, as Illich suggests, their use depends only on the desire to learn.

The fact is that the desire to learn itself cannot be taken for granted and, where it exists, must be channeled. It is a question of who is the subject of education, and in what condition he finds himself.

"A true education," declared the Second Vatican Council, "aims at the formation of the human person in the pursuit of his ultimate end and of the good of the societies of which, as man, he is a member, and in whose obligations, an adult, he will share" (*Gravissimus Educationis*). Or in the words of Pius XI: "The subject of a Christian education is the whole man, spirit united to body in a unity of nature, with all his faculties, natural and supernatural, as he is known through right reason and revelation; that is, man fallen from his original state but redeemed by Christ and reintegrated to the supernatural state of adopted son of God... That is why every pedagogical naturalism which excludes or minimizes the supernatural formation in the instruction of youth is false; and erroneous is every method of education which is founded, totally or partially, in the neglect of original sin and grace and is consequently founded solely on the forces of human nature." Founded solely on the desire to learn, he might have said.

The key to education that takes into account fallen man and grace is authority. Education, if it is to be distinguished from instruction, must fashion man's relation with the world: the whole man with the whole world, natural and supernatural, or better still, natural elevated to the supernatural. That is, there is in education a fundamental element: conformity to reality. This reality must be made present to the student, and this requires authority: the authority of reality itself flowing from the simple fact of its uncontested existence, and the authority of the educator, which influences the student to become what he should be according to his nature. It is not a question of imposition. Rather, to borrow a phrase from Xavier Zubiri, the authority of the educator consists in his being the mouthpiece of things, of reality. The educated man is thus awake to things.

Now, when it is understood that reality includes the supernatural as well as the natural, the question of authority becomes more urgent, for the educator is then the mouthpiece of the Word, the Word of God addressed to man – never an imposition, but an invitation: a free invitation whose simplicity and freedom are the strength of its authority.

Can Illich's learning webs be vessels of this authority? This is the criterion for their viability. But even if they can be, until Christians have enough power over the technological means to try them out, what is the Christian student, the Christian parent to do, now?

After all, conceptualization, however profoundly accurate, of the solution to a problem does not immediately result in elimination of the problem. What is this concrete family to do in the urgent interim?

The Christian has always had to live in two worlds, or better, in two systems: that of grace and that which is an obstacle to grace. By and large the majority of Christians will continue to use the present, un-redeemed system – if only to gain the power to replace it. But steps can be taken now to progress in wisdom while awaiting, or hastening, the moment of liberation.

One such step is the creation of communities, of small units of organically harmonized bonds among family, school and Church. The inhabitants of such educational communities will be about a three-fold activity: first, sharing an academic program in tune with reality, natural and supernatural. Not many disciplines need be involved. Theology, an insight into redemption; philosophy, an insight into being; and history, an insight into action, will suffice. Second, such communities will immerse themselves in a milieu of grace: through the Sacraments, above all the Sacrifice of the Mass, through a personal and communal spiritual direction to make present the depths of the Christian spiritual adventure. These two, integrated, synthesized by the student with the help of the educator, will provide the third activity: the acquisition of a Christian vision which looks outward with a burning desire to bring the Word to all men.

They will be families of believers, these communities – such men as those referred to by Cardinal Wright: men who have seen and heard. They will all, parents, teachers, and children, be students in the school of the Tribe of Christ the King.

It seems proper to end with a plug. All of this is not a dream. Write to this reviewer, at this magazine's address, for information about the Christian Commonwealth Institute.

Padre Pio's Anniversary Mass

Homily: St. Pio of Pietralcina
(The Lord's Gifts are Pure Grace)
On the Second Anniversary
of the Canonization of St. Padre Pio
Church of St. Dominick, Brooklyn, NY
June 15, 2003

It is not only a great joy to join you in this celebration; I do it also in fulfillment of a pledge I made ten years ago to do all I could to promote the knowledge and support for the work of Padre Pio, whom we can publicly call at last what we called him all along, St. Padre Pio.

We knew he was a saint long before the authorities of the Church recognized it. The Italian people overwhelmingly knew he was a saint, and soon the entire world knew it. How so? What was it about him that attracted the millions of followers around the world who recognized in him something that believers and unbelievers alike could call "saintliness" or "holiness"?

I never met Padre Pio during his lifetime. I knew about him, of course. I knew about the strange phenomena associated with him, things like the stigmata and "bi-location," as well as the ability to heal the terminally sick and to read minds and look into the human heart. To tell you the truth, these things kept me away from seeking to find out more about him. I do not understand these things, and although they may be of help to many in their life of faith, they can also lend themselves to an attachment to sensationalism and thus stand in the way of faith. This is indeed the fear of Christ Himself, who told the mob that looked for him that all they wanted was the food he had miraculously provided to them before. And at the time of his passion and death he refused to perform miracles. In any case, he said that not even if a man came back from the dead would those who do not want to believe will not believe. Miracles can strengthen faith, they can point us towards the life that God wants to share with us, but they are not the basis of our faith. The basis for our faith is the attraction of the person of Jesus Christ. Faith begins when we recognize Jesus Christ as the human face of the Mystery for which our hearts were made and without which we cannot be happy and free.

And so it was with Padre Pio. What attracted us to him was not the sensational things associated with his person, but the way his humanity made present to us the attraction of the humanity of Christ. In my case, my devotion to Padre Pio began when I met a man who had met him when he was stationed with the Red Cross near S. Giovanni Rotondo during World War II. My friend, whose name was William Carrigan, heard about the amazing priest at the Capuchin Monastery there and took a group of American soldiers to see what it was all about. Almost fifty years later, Mr. Carrigan could recall and relive the experience of that day. He arrived during Padre Pio's celebration of the Mass, and as he knelt there praying during it, he could not keep his eyes off Padre Pio's face. "I knew it from that very first moment," he said to me. "I knew this man was himself the presence of Christ offering his body and blood for us, for me, for me." On that day after the Mass, Mr. Carrigan met Padre Pio and continued a friendship with him that was to last his entire life. Padre Pio opened his heart to him and told him how much suffering the stigmata and these exceptional phenomena brought him - not physical sufferings, which he was ready to embrace as his share in the sufferings of Christ - but the mental anguish of becoming famous and controversial because of these amazing happiness. Again and again, he told Carrigan, he asked the Lord to remove from him those external demonstrations of his union with Christ. When Mr. Carrigan returned to the United States, he promised Padre Pio that he would dedicate his life to finding him help for his work — in particular, the construction of the Home for the Relief of Suffering for the poor of that region, and the formation of prayer groups for its spiritual support.

Until the end of his life at the age of 97, Mr. Carrigan kept his promise, and his considerable wealth was put at the service of projects that, in his opinion, met with Padre Pio's approval. (An approval that, I believe, was communicated through a privileged spiritual contact that I took for granted without ever trying to understand.) I myself was the beneficiary of Mr. Carrigan and Padre Pio's charity for almost ten years. Mr. Carrigan allowed me to take care of my mother stricken with Alzheimer's disease in a manner following Padre Pio's principles for health care as the "relief of suffering" taking into account the dignity of the patient, including his or her spiritual needs. All of this, he said, because Padre Pio had asked him to help me. During this time I went on a pilgrimage to Padre Pio's tomb to ask him why he had chosen me for this favor and what I could do about it. Nothing spectacular happened on that occasion, but when I left, I knew the answer: the Lord's gifts are pure graces, that is, for no reason at all than the manifestation of the glory of his love, and all that was required of me was to allow that grace to reach others through my particular vocation in life, in this case as a priest. I thanked Padre Pio then, and I asked him that Mr. Carrigan be able to be present at his Beatification. And so indeed it happened, even if by then Carrigan was very sick and very fragile. Still, his family and friends were able to take him on a private plane to Rome and be back in Italy for the first time after he had left at the end of World War II and thus be part of the celebration of the Church's recognition of what he had known all the time: Padre Pio was a saint. He was the manifestation of the Presence of Christ in our world. I knew also that Mr. Carrigan would die before Padre Pio's canonization. For that occasion, they had to be together in heaven, and so indeed it was.

The readings from Sacred Scripture for this Mass will, I believe, help us understand better what it was that attracted Mr. Carrigan and the millions of others who knew, before the Church made it official, that Padre Pio was a saint. Human life is a search for the satisfaction of a desperate desire for happiness, for freedom, for truth, and for beauty. That is what the human being is, this need, this desire is what makes us human, because it shows that we are made for a life that far exceeds our capacity to achieve it through our own efforts. The heart yearns to find the life for which it was made. "Wisdom" is the knowledge of how to look for and find this life. That is why in the first reading today from the Book of Proverbs, Wisdom says:

"My fruit is better than pure gold, my harvest is worth more than the best silver. Happy, the man who listens to me, who watches at my gates day after day, guarding the portals of my entrance. For the one who finds me, finds life, and obtains the favor of God."[1]

Human history is the search for this Wisdom, necessary to obtain the satisfaction of our deepest needs, and necessary to know how to live in order to be really happy, really free. But where is it found, this wisdom? Where does she live? Where are her portals, her gates, the entrance to her home? There is only one way to find the gift of wisdom, namely, to ask for it, to beg it from the Creator of heaven and earth, from the One who made us this way; who made us with this desire for happiness. So great is our desire for it that whenever we meet someone who has found it, we follow him, we become attracted to him, and we yearn

---

1 Proverbs 8:19

to learn this Wisdom from him. This is what attracted millions to Padre Pio. The extraordinary deeds he could perform were not by themselves enough. They were invitations to discover in him a teacher of divine Wisdom. Those who met him, like Mr. Carrigan, recognized this immediately. Padre Pio knew the secret of life. This why he understood so well the human heart. He knew the needs of the heart. When we cannot find the fulfillment that our hearts desire, then we suffer. Suffering is more than a physical or emotional pain. Suffering is a spiritual pain. It is the loss of the meaning of human life. It is the loss of wisdom. That is why Padre Pio recognized that the relief of the suffering of the sick requires more than physical or emotional help. It requires the experience of a love that restores to us the experience of the goodness and value of life. It requires the experience of a share in the Wisdom that reveals the secret of why we were created and the ultimate meaning of what we are experiencing. That is why he is a saint, and not because of the stigmata or because of bi-location, or other such phenomena. He was a saint because he had opened his heart to divine wisdom and shared it lovingly with those who were suffering.

Divine wisdom is not intellectual knowledge. It is a knowledge of the heart that arises from wonder at the greatness and beauty of God, and at the infinity of his mercy and love. Only the one who loves finds and possesses wisdom. In today's reading from the Gospel of Matthew, Jesus thanks the Father for revealing his secrets. Jesus thanks the Father for communicating his wisdom; not to the learned, the wise, or the powerful, but to the "little ones" of the world, to those whose hearts are like the hearts of children, expecting all as a gift of the Father's love. This "purity of heart," as the Lord calls it in the Sermon of the Mount, is what allows us to see God. This purity of heart is the key to the possession of Wisdom, giving us the strength to bear anything that can happen to us in this life. This purity of heart gives meaning and value to our sufferings, and transforms them into acts of love. Love is that "light burden" and "sweet yoke" of which Jesus speaks. Love is available to those whose heart is "humble," who are willing to receive wisdom as a gift, and do not attempt to be the authors of what is good or bad, true or false. The words of the Lord describe his own heart, as he says it himself: "Learn from me." Jesus Christ is the revelation of Divine Wisdom, and Padre Pio possessed it because he had received it and learned it from Christ. It was Christ in Him that attracted the hearts of the millions who followed Padre Pio seeking the same gift for themselves.

And how was it that Padre Pio received this divine Wisdom, this presence of Christ in his own heart? He did so by following Christ always, by traveling the way of the cross of Christ that leads to wisdom and true life, exposing the great error of those who think themselves wise by their own efforts. "Come to me, all of you who are tired and overburdened," He said, whose search for wisdom has been futile, unable to satisfy the desires of your heart. Padre Pio came to Him, gave Himself entirely to Him, and thus became the way for millions who followed Christ with him and in him. Padre Pio personified the following of Christ as St. Paul described it in today's second reading from the letter to the Galatians:

"As for me, I bear in my body the very signs of Christ."[2]

This is what matters in life. This is the secret of love, the secret of life. This is our Wisdom, and not the wisdom of the world that depends on power and violence, or on the observance of laws that we have no power to observe except by crushing our desires for happiness and fullness of life.

This is what we celebrate today, pledging to follow Christ's path outlined to us by Padre Pio. May he obtain for us in heaven at the side of Christ who is God's Wisdom, the joy of walking along this path today in gratitude for the love he showed for us, making of us apostles for the relief of suffering in a world so desperately in need for love.

---

2 Galatians 6:17

Education and Mystery

TRACES Magazine
2000

G.K. Chesterton regretted that it had taken him too long to realize that there is no such thing as education! That is a great consolation to me, since for the last 28 years I have been trying to figure out what I thought about it. It all began with an invitation to Australia back in 1971. I had written a review of a book by the controversial educator Ivan Illich (formerly "Monsignor" Illich) in which he called for a revamping of the whole educational enterprise by substituting "educational networks" for the schools, since these had lost their roots in a harmonious alliance between the family, the Church, and the State. That, as far as I can remember, was more or less his argument. I remember that I agreed with his argument, but criticized the networks he proposed as artificial, arguing that education could only occur within a community of persons that shared a common experience of the meaning of life. Or something like that, anyway. The point is that I was really talking off the top of my head since I was forced to do a review about a subject about which I really knew nothing.

Apparently, I must have said something that impressed a group of educators in Australia because they wrote to me inviting me to participate in some kind of congress, all expenses paid plus a nice honorarium. I desperately wanted to accept this opportunity for a nice, free trip, but I was afraid that they would quickly discover that I knew nothing about education! And so I thought and thought about what I could say that would impress them, but failed totally to come up with any idea beyond what I had written for the review. I declined the invitation, but all these years I have been troubled by my inability to figure what education really is. That is why I was so happy to read that Chesterton concluded that there is no such thing. No wonder I had all that trouble.

Education comes from the Latin term for "leading out of..." Education is not a "thing"; it is an action, a method of liberation. The question is: what is being liberated through the action called education? Some say that education is the "leading out of the student" of what is somehow trapped within him, as opposed to "instruction" which seeks to "put something into" the student that was not there. In the name of this "leading out of," educators have designed methods to "release the potential" within the students, helping them to be "authentic" to their deepest self. The problem with this view can be seen in the abysmal ignorance and incompetence of graduates from institutions that have embraced this approach. They are authentic indeed, embarrassingly so, authentically ignorant. Those who realize it suffer and are condemned to a life at the margins of society. Those who do not realize it become intolerably — and dangerously — selfish.

But if education is different from instruction, if it is really a "leading out of... "What is it exactly that is led out and from where ... and more important, where to? (Once we know this, we can figure out just who is equipped to do the leading out, who the real educators are.)

It seems to me that what is led out is the student... not what is within him (or her, to be politically correct), but the person of the students. One presumably educates persons. Indeed this is what distinguishes education from "instruction." Instruction is an element, a part of education, but one educates only persons, whereas one can instruct dogs. Students are led out of what? I suppose one can say, "out of ignorance," where ignorance refers not just to lack of skills or information, but an insufficient grasp of reality. Education occurs through an encounter with reality, an encounter that sets the student free. Only such an encounter can be educative. The educator is the one who facilitates this encounter through instruction, gesture, and witness. The student is led out of ignorance to a deeper and deeper penetration into reality.

This is possible if reality itself is experienced as always pointing to deeper and deeper levels of life, *only if reality is experienced as a sign.* It is this experience that is properly educative, formative: the experience of an exceptional dimension of reality, namely, its orientation to a Mystery that fills up the emptiness of the heart, the needs of the heart. The heart is originally poor with that "original solitude" or "original poverty" that is man's initial condition from which he yearns to be set free; a thirst, a desperate need, a hunger, a radical dependence, a demand. Education is thus the very opposite of setting free what is in the heart; it is the way the heart is pointed towards the Mystery that alone can fulfill it. Education is redemptive. The Educator, the Teacher can only be the Redeemer of the heart.

Mass at St. Joseph's Seminary

Homily
March 20, 2001

The Christian faith is not the result of religious, ethical, or philosophical speculation. It is always the result of an encounter; of something that happens to us. It happens to us in ordinary ways, through the concrete circumstances of our lives. This is how "Revelation" reaches us. A revelation reaches us not through words alone, but through words and circumstances; through circumstances that become a Word addressed to us. A Word that indicates the Presence of Christ with us. It is as if each one of us had to go through our own little Incarnations for us and to us: the Word becomes flesh for us means the Word becomes circumstances for us. The circumstances of our lives. The concrete circumstances through which we are passing at each moment in our lives, that is the flesh of the Incarnation that occurs for us. Just as Mary's body and circumstances – her engagement to Joseph, for example, as well as her virginity – became the body of Christ. Just as Mary's body and circumstances were the flesh which the Eternal Son made his own body in order to enter into our world, becomes the body of Christ. Just so, the concrete circumstances of our lives, our own life in the flesh, becomes the body of Christ.

I am saying this because it seems to me that it would be an inexcusable flight into abstraction if I would concentrate in this little homily on the readings without any reference to the way that God's Word has been proclaimed to us in this seminary community. This past week, God's Word has been communicated through the changes in our circumstances announced by Cardinal Egan last Thursday. This change in our circumstances should not be separated from the Word that the Lord is addressing to us. Our Marian faith must turn this change in our circumstances into an Incarnation for us. Our faith must turn these circumstances into an encounter with Christ, with his Presence in our circumstances, seeking to turn them into his Body. The Holy Spirit is the One that brings this about, just as in the Incarnation of the Lord in Mary's body and circumstances. Don Luigi Giussani teaches us who follow his charism a little prayer to say throughout the day for this purpose. Permit me to commend it to you in what may be the last time I speak to all of you in this context. The prayer recites the phrase: "Veni Sancte Spiritus, Veni per Mariam. Come Holy Spirit, come through Mary." We are praying for the Incarnation to occur for us through the concrete circumstances through which we are passing. Think of how the prayer in our first reading seeks to turn the circumstances through which the people of God were passing:

"Now we have no prince, nor chief, nor prophet, nor holocaust, nor sacrifice, nor offering, nor incense, nor place in which to offer to you our first fruits and obtain mercy."

These are pretty negative and depressing circumstances, I must say. But this is turned into a privileged opportunity for the encounter with God to take place; for Revelation to take place; for an experience of God's mercy to be greater than what they knew before. And in the gospel, we have the opposite: the case of a man who does not recognize what happens to him. The man does not recognize the change in circumstances. He does not see that the experience of his monstrous debt being forgiven is a revelation that could and should have changed his heart. He does not recognize that he could become himself the body of forgiveness to those who owed him much less. When our circumstances change, as ours did last week, it is the time to recognize this change. When our circumstances change we should see it as an encounter with Christ. How else can an encounter take place if it doesn't alter our circumstances? This is what makes it an encounter. Our faith, as we saw, is based on the encounter with Christ in the flesh of our circumstances. If not, it becomes pure abstraction, pure theory, and pure speculation.

The Eucharist we celebrate is the perfect embodiment of the prayer, "Veni Sancte Spiritus, Veni per Mariam." Let us so celebrate it on the altar and encounter the sacramental Christ, so that we can celebrate it in our changed circumstances, with absolutely the same results. "Let that celebration 'be our sacrifice,' and may it be perfect in your Presence, because those who trust in you are never defrauded."

Mass On the Occasion of Fr. Giussani's Death

Homily
Holy Family Church, NYC
February 22, 2005

It is important to know that there has never been a type of Christianity that did not originally express itself in the form of a ritual. The rite was an integral part of the expression of the primitive Church and of its life in communion. The rite was an expression of the reality of a new life when a social group was constituted and distinguished by a new form of ritual. The Eucharist, which in the Greek means the giving of thanks, was the mark of the community's whole life in those early times. And so, early Christians did what Christ had asked them to do. They followed his example just before he was taken prisoner and killed. They followed him in the gesture and sign that held all the ontological density of the real presence of Jesus. It was called sacrament, while in the Greek it meant mystery. While this Mystery does maintain its infinite content, it also in some ways reveals itself in our finite state. The Mystery makes itself a part of our experience...as we live it, and it makes itself known to our senses. Christ is the Mystery itself for the very reason that He is God who makes of himself a human experience. He is the infinite Word that became man. A man that we can listen to, see, and touch.

These are the words of Monsignor Luigi Giussani in his book *Why the Church.* Those of us around the world are learning to live our humanity the way Giussani lived his by studying together in our schools of community. For us, the Mystery that Christ is became also in Father Giussani. A man we could listen to, see, and touch. For Father Giussani himself, the sacramental veil of the Mystery has now been finally lifted. The experience of Giussani's humanity is, we believe, now a perfect experience of our oneness with Christ. This reality, which is now entirely his life, we have come to experience through our senses tonight. We do this as Giussani taught us to celebrate the Eucharist. In so doing, we believe that we already begin to experience now, in this life, the life that our Father Giussani now lives at the center of its origin. We begin to experience in all the aspects of our present life, in this world, that life. We begin to experience in all circumstances and relationships the life that Father Giussani now lives: the God who makes of himself a human experience in Jesus Christ. For this reason, paradoxically, the pain of our separation from him becomes, through the sacrifice of Christ offered through this Eucharist, the very bond that brings us together in the victory over this very separation. Father Giussani has never been closer to us. This is not merely an intellectual conviction, but an experience in this world. An experience in our flesh and through our senses.

Even the day in which Father Giussani entered eternity is in complete harmony with his life and charism. Today when he reached the full truth of his and our human life, the Church celebrates the feast of the Chair of Peter. Today the Church celebrates the continuing mission of the Apostle Peter to be the sign of the unity of the Church, and the unity upon which the future of the world depends. As a priest, Father Giussani's human words and gestures were the means through which Peter and the apostles exercise from heaven that care for us. This is heard in the Preface of the Mass which gives thanks always and everywhere. At their side now, Father Giussani will continue to exercise this care and maybe help Peter understand the meaning of his yes. Father Giussani might even have a lesson or two for Andrew and John!

We are honored and privileged to have with us tonight the representative of the Holy Father to the United Nations, Archbishop Celestino Migliore. He makes concrete the service which the Chair of Peter offers to a world searching for unity, justice, and peace. The Church is indeed an expert in humanity, and offers to the world the service on behalf of human dignity and authentic freedom that flows from her identity as the manifestation of Christ's victory. That is why Father Giussani was so happy, so moved, so thrilled, and so grateful for the opportunity to present his book *The Religious Sense*[1] at the United Nations. The religious sense is the grammar of what it means to be a human person. And to think that this presentation was followed by the presentation of *At the Origin of the Christian Claim*. Father Giussani made the United Nations headquarters a public forum. He turned it into a kind of Solomon's Portico of the world where he could give witness to our experience of Christ as the one without which the efforts to live our humanity to the fullness are in vain! Your Excellency, thank you for being with us and giving us the opportunity to reaffirm the commitment we learned from Father Giussani. Thank you for helping the Chair of Peter give this witness to the world. The presentation of *The Religious Sense* at the United Nations marked the beginning of a miraculous growth for the Movement here in the United States. This too brought a great joy to Father Giussani. He loved our country. He loved its passion for the ideal of freedom, and its commitment to facilitate everyone's pursuit of happiness. He loved the creativity, the imagination, and the passion with which these ideals were pursued in this country. On the very first day I met him he spoke of the fertile soil that this land offers to the gospel. Here he saw a fruitful soil that can overcome the weeds of ideological thinking. Weeds that can distort this American dream. Father Giussani bore a great love for the history of American Protestantism and saw it as a crucial component of this country's simple hope in the

---

1 Giussani, Luigi; The Religious Sense; Montreal, Canada; Mc-Gill-Queen's University Press; 1997.

possibilities for the success of the human adventure. Father Giussani said to me that he wanted our Movement to sink its roots in American soil and grow as an American plant. We are those roots now, and we joyfully embrace this task before us, remembering that it is to be pursued entirely by a Marian opening to grace.

This is our contribution: the presence, the intercession, the freedom, and the total abandonment of Mary to the Holy Spirit. This is how we are faithful to the incredible and undeserved privilege of being the fruits of Father Giussani's virginal paternity. We are faithful by living every moment of our lives as a plea; a prayer. We are the embodiment of the prayer he taught us: "Come Holy Spirit; come through Mary." May Our Lady bring our Father Giussani at last to the vision of the infinite beauty of the glory of Christ, and lead us to be with him at the vanishing point that is our destiny with Christ.

From Evangelization to Education

TRACES Magazine
On Deus Caritas Est
2006

Pope Benedict XVI's first encyclical, *Deus Caritas Est*[1] is the logical follow up to John Paul II' s effort of evangelization. If in a certain way John Paul offered us the content of the Church's message, Pope Benedict points us to the method, namely, an *education in love*.

Although never mentioned explicitly, this encyclical is in many ways a response to the Theology of Liberation that proposed a Marxist analysis of society as the basis for a Christian humanism. *Deus Caritas Est* proposes the Church's *ministry of charity* to be an education of the human heart in love as the way to respond to the drama of the contemporary need for justice in this world. In that sense, the encyclical is a reflection and deepening

---

1 The Supreme Pontiff Benedict XVI; Encyclical Letter Deus Caritas Est, On Christian Love; 2005; http://w2.vatican.va/content/benedict-xvi/en/encyclicals/documents/hf_ben-xvi_enc_20051225_deus-caritas-est.html

of the appeal for education that says that if there was an education of the people, everybody would live better.

But for Pope Benedict, charity's power is not that of an external, ethical inspiration. Charity transforms the human heart itself which is the source of our judgments and actions. The Church's contribution to the struggle for a better world is an education of the heart in charity. At the very beginning of the second part of the encyclical, Pope Benedict underlines the centrality of the gift of the Holy Spirit that is the fruit of Christ's redemption of the world. This Spirit harmonizes the human heart with Christ's heart and moves it to love as Christ loves.[2] We have here an echo of the Patristic view of the history of salvation as the education of man's heart to divine life, and of God's heart, so to speak, to human life. This is the education of *eros* to *agape* and of *agape* to *eros*. This education by the Spirit *transforms the heart* of the ecclesial community. The evangelization of the world through Word and Sacrament becomes in this way a force that promotes man in the various arenas of life and human activity. This service or ministry of charity is thus essential to the nature of the Church, and its power is educative. This service is the presence of Christ through Word and Sacrament which becomes an energy for change in the condition of human life in this world. There is absolutely no dualism here. Through this education in charity Christ and his redemptive work are made present within human history. Christ creates a new human history through the transformation of the

---

2 cf., p.19

heart. This education in charity is the method through which evangelization becomes an event in human history. Without this method the gospel remains an abstraction and nothing really changes. The principle of subsidiarity, which is so central to the Church's social doctrine, is thus not much more than just an ethical principle. It expresses a consequence of the Incarnation.

Although the Church's ministry of charity is different from the State's obligation to pursue social justice, the education in love offered by the ministry of charity also contributes to the pursuit of justice by the effect it has on human reason. With this insistence Pope Benedict again responds to the position of those theologies of social justice that would uncritically embrace an analysis and judgment about the concrete demands of justice separated from the experience of faith. Such an analysis must be indeed the work of reason, but as an educative reality the ministry of charity has an impact on reason itself.

The problem of justice is indeed a problem of practical reason, but, Pope Benedict says:

"If reason is to be exercised properly, it must undergo constant purification, since it can never be completely free of the danger of a certain ethical blindness caused by the dazzling effects of power and special interests."[3]

---

3 The Supreme Pontiff Benedict XVI; Encyclical Letter Deus Caritas Est, On Christian Love; 2005; p. 28; http://w2.vatican. va/content/benedict-xvi/en/encyclicals/documents/hf_ben-xvi_ enc_20051225_deus-caritas-est.html

Indeed, at this point "politics and faith meet." This statement of Pope Benedict will certainly disturb those - including Catholics, and especially Catholic politicians - that insist on a radical separation between their faith and their political life. Again and again Pope Benedict insists on the fact that the Church does not get involved in politics as such, and that non-Christians have nothing to fear from the Church's proposals concerning the demands of justice. It is absolutely true that faith by its specific nature is an encounter with the living God; an encounter opening up new horizons extending beyond the sphere of reason. But it is also a purifying force for reason itself. Faith "liberates reason from its blind spots and therefore helps it to be ever more fully itself." The "purification of reason" is thus not an imposition to nonbelievers of "ways of thinking and modes of conduct proper to faith". The purification of reason occurs within the "autonomous sphere of reason" itself and can be verified by reason. This conviction of the Church is the *risk* of education.

What Are You Looking For?

Lecture at a Priest Retreat
March 24-28, 2008

Introduction

I will begin with a question that is of great importance
to all of us, to the method of Father Giussani, but which
is also a normal question, namely: What am I looking
for? Why am I coming to this retreat? What do I expect?
What do we want out of this week? All during this entire
week, in all our conversations, to reflect on what we are
reflecting on, we must have this question in mind. We
must constantly ask ourselves why we are here. Some
of you are new. There must be some reason why you
have come to this, not knowing many of us (or any of
us) or anything about Communion and Liberation. Why
did you come, especially after a busy and tiring week?
I wouldn't be surprised if some say, "Oh, I've had
enough! Next week I want to go slow in all this spiritual
stuff." Those of you who are old-timers at this…you are
back. Why? What are you looking for? These, in fact,
are the first words of the Word of God Incarnate in the
Gospel of St. John. This question must be important,

because in St. John, as you know, the reality of, the concept of the Word of God is crucial—central—to his Gospel. The *Logos*—the reason, the meaning, the purpose of the existence of anything, is the Logos—the philosophical term taken from Greek thought. It's what gives value and sense to life; it's the rationality of life. If we didn't have an experience of this, for example, then we could not complain about injustice. Why complain? Because there is no reason for anything that happens—starting with one's own existence. Your existence is but an accident of the great evolutionary scheme of things, that moves on without any particular direction or purpose. There is no rationality. That which gives rationality to reality, so that things are supposed to make sense, that is the *Logos*... the Word, the Word of God. And so, the amazing thing about the Gospel of St. John is that this *Logos*—how does one say it in any other way—became a human being. This *Logos* acquired a face with a humanity like ours: eyes, ears, nose, throat. So Rationality itself is going to speak.

In this Gospel, the very first words of Jesus, the very first words of the Mystery to those two, John and Andrew, who approached Him after whatever happened at the "John the Baptist Show," the very first words are: "What do you want? What are you looking for?" They are kind of stalking Him; curious—something is attracting them. They hardly know anything about Him except some stuff about "Lamb of God" which they overheard John saying. Whatever it is, they move in His direction. So Jesus stops and looks at them and says the first words that the Logos speaks in John's Gospel.

"What are you looking for? What do you want?" It seems to me that this recommends itself as an important question, because the rest of the Gospel is going to be an interplay between the answer to this question and Christ. Christ presenting Himself, identifying Himself as that which fulfills those desires. But, if we are not familiar with those desires or haven't really thought it through, then we cannot recognize the value of whatever it is that Jesus offers to us. So I think Christian life— and before we are priests, we are Christians—is lived in the relationship between those two questions: "What are you looking for?" and "What do you want?" We know their answer was really amazing and, in a certain sense, understandable because they knew nothing about Jesus. They knew nothing about His teaching or values, His way of looking at life, or His claims. Whatever was attracting them was His company, because they say, "We want to find out where You are. We want to be with You." Where You remain. You don't disappear. You're not just passing by. We want a place where we can be together. It's an interesting answer, before they have any particular questions, and I'm sure they had many. The first one was as simple as that: "We want to be with You. There is something that attracts us to You." So how can we be like You? His answer was, "Follow Me." Come with Me. Walk with Me. I'm not going to stay put in a particular place; I'm going to be running around. Come run with Me.

This question is also reflected, as Pope Benedict notes in *Spe Salvi*, in the Liturgy of Baptism, by the first two questions. The questions from a certain perspective are stupid (unless you baptize anything that walks in). You already have the certificate filled out, but you ask, "What name do you give your child?" One could respond, "What are you talking about? Read the paper!" The question is, "What do you want?" This reminds me of my first confession, when I realized I would not be a new John Vianney. Soon after being ordained, I sat down in the confessional (getting a little claustrophobic, but I thought to myself, "It's worth it; let me find out what people are really doing"). The first man who came in began with, "I don't know why I'm here." At that time, I didn't realize that he was really a mystic, because he was addressing the real question. "What am I doing here?" At that time, I thought he was stupid. I said, "I hope you don't want a Big Mac with fries, because you have made a great mistake." He started laughing uncontrollably; you could hear it all over the church. People started moving to other confessionals. He said that he didn't mean that, and he said why he was there, and what made him enter the church to begin with, and, "You are going to hear things, Father, that you never heard before." I said, "That's not going to be too difficult; this is my very first confession!" So I always thought in the Liturgy of Baptism, "Why start this way?" But as the pope says in *Spe Salvi*, it is the same question, because that is the beginning of the journey. It is going to be like the journey of those apostles. For some reason, you are before Christ, and here, someone else, someone who loves you, is confronted with the question: "What name do you give your child?" Is there anything more personal than a name? Who you are, not just what you are. The name you give your child… The child is the what. The name is the who. You answer as best as you can—the child has no awareness of what's going on. But you, who love this child, and in some way live in the child, and the child in you, you know what is going on. What is the name you give, how do you know this child? It is something that engages the very self; one's identity. And then: "What do you ask of the Church?" In the ritual that is quoted by the pope, the suggested answer is: "Faith." The third question is: "What does faith give to you?" Why do you want faith? And the answer that is suggested is: "Eternal Life." We follow Christ because we want eternal life, because with Him as companion or with ourselves as His companions, we begin to taste something of what we call (for lack of a better term), Eternal Life. That is why we are here, I hope. What is this Eternal Life? How do you understand this and why should you want it? We must answer, honestly, the question: "What are you looking for?"

What do you want for yourself, not only of this week, but of your life? Your life as human. What do you want so that you can have some satisfaction, for however long it is, (and it is always too short), of one's passage through existence? If, at the end, you want to pass a judgment on yourself, what would make you have a positive judgment on your life? What is the value of your life? Would you not want something at least to have been accomplished? If this question concerns our human existence as such, it also concerns our reality, our existence as believers, as followers of Christ, but also our lives as priests. What do we want? This is a good self-question for these days. And then, when you confront it, the next question is: How do you believe that it is possible? How do you propose to get what you want? Why do you think that what you want exists any place? These are questions that, even if we don't ask them consciously, are still within us. And unless they are dealt with this way, in total honesty with ourselves, they will always be there somehow draining us from a life that we could, yes, enjoy. We could find satisfaction in it. The question is there—it is a question in the human heart, if you wish. It is decisive. That is why it is useful to bring it up to consciousness, and see where we are.

I have found, and suggest to you, that if you do not live within the context of this question, everything that we might take out of this week will be entirely theoretical and abstract and will change nothing. Nothing will change in you, or in those to whom you minister, and it will eventually diminish until it's gone. Only if we remain attached to that question will these things change something; make a difference. This was one of Father Giussani's fundamental concerns, and we never tire of going back to it again and again. It is decisive. We risk everything on this point. Without living this, within the environment of this question, outside of that everything will make us enthusiastic for a while, but in the end, it becomes boring, repetitive, and tasteless. You just hang in because it's too late to start anything new. It changes nothing. It's like reading a pagan author about a pagan liturgy. Impressive ceremonies again and again and again, but nothing happens. At most, there is a little inspiring shot, but it won't survive.

So, how do I know what I want? I don't know. To be with Jesus. Faith. More faith. Eternal Life. I don't know ultimately how this is related to me, to my fundamental and original desires. You can try to go deeper and deeper in a very noble way but, in the end, I must tell you that I find only one thing: I just want to have a good time. Yes. See, I don't suspect I'm lying when I say that. When I say, "I want a life of love and justice!" That's fine. But it's more. And I am told and helped and trained to listen to myself. You yourself are the first person you minister to. How do I listen to my heart? In life there are so many adjustments, so many compromises; you seek so many distractions, undergo so many resignations. You don't have the power to cut through all that and find the original defining desires of your heart. I cannot. That would really be the most honest answer: I don't know. I don't know what I want. I don't know how to read my heart. Something has to happen to me. Something happens, it awakens me to the desires that are there. Something that will touch where my desires are, that will really strike me, and impact me with a reality that hits me right there, where my identity begins. It invades my entire humanity like an injection that spreads its liquid through the entire body and affects everything. When that happens, then I awaken. It has to be something that is truly exceptional because I am impacted by many things in a day, but I am used to them. It has to be something exceptional. That is the key word Father Giussani uses. There is a name, a word, a terminology, that describes the kind of event that awakens the heart and is therefore a privileged way of finding out what I want. That word is encounter. I need an encounter to awaken me, to give me energy, and to clarify what I am looking at and what I am looking for. Many of us are like the drunk man who is looking for the keys to his car near the lamp post. He didn't lose them there, he lost them four blocks away, but there was more light at this place, so he thought he would start there. Something that is exceptional...

It's Easter Monday. Easter was yesterday. It feels like it was seven months ago. The disciples at Emmaus lasted a lifetime compared to me and how long my Easter enthusiasm lasted. You get all moved, shaken up (if at all), when you engage in the celebration, but how long does it last? And we are the priests! People are supposed to get it from us. Get what? Two days later, the disciples on the way to Emmaus said, "We had hoped..." We had hoped, but now that hope is rapidly going away. Love grows cold, says the Scripture. If not even the Resurrection of Jesus can survive this, what can I expect? What kind of event must happen? What kind of encounter is necessary to sustain us in this way? The Resurrection of Jesus does not do it because, for many of us, that was an event in the past and we have never seen anything like it. We believe it. But what does it mean that Jesus of Nazareth rose from the dead? The people I love haven't popped out again. Even when I consider my own faith, there is nothing in me that assures me. It is too abstract. When we talk about the Resurrection of Jesus, what are we talking about? If you do not talk about something that has happened to you, and that you have seen and heard and, as the Evangelist says, touched with your hand, smelled with your nose, heard with your ear, then why talk about it? Something great must happen, and by great, I don't mean in terms of a great spectacle, but something that I can identify, that is astounding. In fact, I am used to great spectacles. If it is an astounding display—with a huge fire in the heavens saying, "Jesus is Risen!" —it will not last! It has to happen in here, it has to touch and change something in me. I need that. I would say to Jesus, "I can't even answer your question, 'What are you looking for?'" You tell me. That is what I want, I guess. To be with You, so that You can tell me what I want. Because outside of this, nothing else will convince me or change me or mean anything—unless I decide to live by abstraction or theories. Nothing else will change me, even the most spectacular, the most satisfying gifts one can give me.

Thinking about politics before the election, we are reminded of the story by Vladimir Soloviev, *A Short Tale of the Anti-Christ.*[1] It is the story of this leader that surfaces. He beings to serve the public, he runs for office, etc. By the middle of the story, he has succeeded in everything. He has united the world.

---

1 Solovyov, Vladimir; War, Progress, and the End of History: Three Conversations, Including a Short Tale of the Antichrist (Esalen-Lindisfarne Library of Russian Philosophy); Great Barrington, MA; Lindisfarne Books, Anthroposophic Press, Steiner Books; 1990

He has things going that satisfy all the needs of the world, material and spiritual. He's a very religious man (also a vegetarian). He was also kind and gentle to animals. It all really worked—except for a band of hard-nosed Christians who didn't go along. Of all the Christian denominations, most followed him. He didn't claim any religious title; he respected all religions; he gave absolute religious unity; he gave assistance to the churches. But what he wanted now was to go to this remaining group and invite them to join. He wanted to bring unity. So they are summoned, and they go to the Leader. In fact, the pope presides over this small flock. (There is also a Protestant and Orthodox leader.) They are not threatened with persecution, and the Leader asks them the same question: "What do you want?" What can I give you so that you can join everybody else in this satisfaction? They don't answer; they look at each other. Finally, the decisive moment comes. He says (and I am reading the actual text):

"Tell me yourselves, Christians, abandoned by the majority of your brothers and sisters and leaders, condemned by popular sentiment. What do you find most precious in Christianity? Tell me. What is most precious to you, so that I can contribute to it and you can join me?"

And then one of them replies, (and it says in the text, "with sweetness."):

"Great sovereign! That which we have of most value in Christianity is Christ Himself. He Himself, and

everything that comes from Him. Because we know that in Him dwells bodily, the fullness of divinity. From you sovereign, we are prepared to receive any good, but only if in your generous hand, we can recognize the holy hand of Christ. And in answer to your questions, what you can do for us, this is our precise response: Confess in front of us, Jesus Christ, Son of God Incarnate, who was risen from the dead, who will come again. Confess, and we will embrace you with profound love as the true of His coming."

What we value the most, our treasure, is Jesus Christ. Is it true? Let's think about it in these days, but for this to happen, we need the Holy Spirit, so let us begin by singing, "Come, Holy Spirit."

Lesson One

For so many people, this morning has not been the kind of morning the song says. It's been another morning of despair (to evoke sentimentality here). Realistically speaking, many do not have the advantage of being here together like this. I would like them to have such a morning. Among the many things, the answer to my question — "What are you looking for?"— is part of it. I'm looking for a life in which these divisions do not exist—that some people have a morning like this, and are led to praise God, and that others don't, and are led to damn Him maybe or at least to be disillusioned, or feel rejected in some way. We all know people we love in such a situation.

So what are you looking for? I'm looking for a life in which this is not so. If the Lord wants to engage me in conversation, that's an attempt at an answer for Him.

Another thing I noticed here, that runs through this, is the amazing —and I use the word used by Father Giussani, stolen from Charles Péguy — the *carnality* of it. When we first started these retreats, on Easter Monday down in St. Augustine, Florida, prior to beginning the first morning session, I went for a little walk. I was thinking about how, in a sense, this must have been there: the river, the trees, and all that, on the very first Easter morning. And I was remembering about how the psalms that we say all week long make reference to all Creation jumping out of control—the clouds and the sky. This is amazing, that nature participates in the Resurrection of Christ. I asked myself: "Is this a figure of speech, a poetic way of speaking, or did something happen that morning?" Had the Resurrection of Christ really changed this world in its roots? I don't know what time the Resurrection occurred, but this is what we believe, that it was a point in our time. It is an event that surpasses anything that we have known or can know, but at least it occurred in this world. So there was a certain time in which He had not risen, and a time in which He had risen. The Resurrection is not a manifestation of His triumph and return to the Father, it is an event in His life, an event in the life of Jesus in this world; it occurs in this world. According to our songs and psalms, all of nature, all of Creation rejoices. Now, I could ask the trees, you can go ask them now.

(Well, this is San Francisco, it may enhance our reputation if we talk to trees). How does Creation participate in these things?

St. Paul, who was not necessarily known as being a leader of the Green Party, nonetheless says that all of creation is yearning for what happened in us, what happens in us, in the Resurrection. In what way is it yearning? Again, if this is poetic, in which case it is theoretical, in which case it changes nothing. You might as well believe in the resurrection of the Great Lizard. If it inspires you as much as that of Jesus, take the lizard, if it is a matter of only inspiring. Not with those people whose morning is not this one. Inspiration is not going to get them out of their hell. Then what is it? What happens? Whatever it is, O dear Jesus, that's what I am looking for. It is my answer to the question, at least initially. Perhaps less faith-developed than that of the apostles, John and Andrew, who at least said, "We want to be with You." I don't even mention Him in my answer. But I want to be with Him, if being with Him leads to this. I can put it that way, as honestly as I can. Because if it doesn't lead to what happens in us in the Resurrection, if I cannot learn to recognize Him, and love Him, and want to be with Him, and fall in love with Him, and acknowledge His beauty through this, then how? By having my favorite picture by some favorite artist in my imagination? Look, I'm opening myself. It's there. All the years of theology, I appreciate it, I love this material. I love J. A. Ratzinger, von Balthasar, and John Paul II. It's great, and I'm for it, and all they say is true, but unless something like that occurs in my flesh (to use the Biblical word), then how can I say it's true? I can say it's a beautiful vision. It's intellectually cohesive, it's inspiring, but is it true? Can I risk everything? Because as we know, the demand is for everything, whatever one's vocation. Can I risk everything on such a wonderful, beautiful view of things? I need something more, if the risking of everything is going to be a joy and not an act of surrender of some kind. Because, after all, who am I before the God, the Mystery that created all things? "I have fallen in love with whatever was there before the Big Bang." Come on, that's crazy. Try Sylvia or whatever turns you on. The carnality of it. The question, "What are you looking for?" is addressed to the heart, and that means, to the carnal self. Whatever the answer is, and whatever is offered to us, must have this concrete reality. A reality where I am united with it in such a way that I am a living witness to that reality, and I am only that. Because if it doesn't occur like this, then we are still living things with the one thing that will paralyze us and get us nowhere, and that is dualism.

Dualism (and you are lucky there is only two; most of us have "ten-ism"), that is, identities that we have. That is why Father Giussani has said, and Carrón keeps insisting, that at the very first moment, on the morning that you get up, you throw in the Angelus. Because this is about the only moment in which you still haven't put on the first mask, and you wonder what's there. Confront that with the Angelus, as an event that occurred to this woman. One of the phrases of Father Giussani as a theologian that affected me the most, is a quote from John Paul II (and stolen from Vatican II). The phrase is that Christ is the center of history and the universe. That turned me on. Father Giussani said that, yes, of course, Christ is the center of history and the universe, but before that, he was a lump of blood in the womb of a Jewish girl. The center of history and the universe, it's a beautiful concept; it is true when said of Christ. But it is just a concept. A lump of blood is not. That is the affirmation. In fact, there was an international catechetical congress in November 2003 in Rome, and Father Giussani sent a message that begins with one of the great quotes from Péguy: "Ego sum via, veritas, et vita. The words of life, the living words must be maintained alive, must be nourished with life. You must take this word and nourish it. Bear it. Heat it up in your living heart. Do not just take them and conserve them in little boxes of wood. Like Jesus has done, He was forced to take a body, to dress Himself with flesh in order to pronounce these carnal words and make us understand them"— in order to be able to pronounce them with a human voice. If I don't hear a human voice... There are people who claim (they could be lying), that they fell madly in love with someone they had just met on the Internet. They hadn't heard a thing; they hadn't talked on the phone. I want someone standing there, so I can hear the voice without props. If I am going to hand myself over entirely—entirely—without reservation, I need this. I love the idea that Christ took on flesh, had to, in a sense, had to, in order to reach us. He had to in order to address us and pronounce the words, so we could hear a human voice pronounce the words. He was constrained to take on a body to pronounce the words.

Giussani said that we must do the same. Those of us who are flesh must profit from this. From the fact that we are flesh, so that we can conserve these words. So we can nourish them. So that we can derive carnal life from it. These words were used by Father Giussani to address an activity in which we all, in one way or another, have catechetical responsibilities. This is important. If you have found another method that works, and endures, and satisfies you, then speak out. But I don't know any other. And we all know pastorally what that may be. You might have an excellent program that works well while the person is in the program (sometimes even then it doesn't work well), but the person is not going to be in the program forever. And what happens when they leave? What happens when their flesh wakes up? And I don't mean just sex, but their *worldliness*—let's use that word, because flesh is worldliness. What's wrong with worldliness? On the contrary, I don't like other-worldly people. Once we live worldliness, what happens with the method or whatever they learned in catechism? Well, we know what happens. We have today the greatest Catholic population in the leadership of the United States at all levels: government, media, business, etc. Has it made any difference? We really have a physically-Catholic presence. That is a fact in this country, which we would have never imagined before. How many judges in the Supreme Court are

Catholic, etc.? Chris Matthews and Tim Russert are Catholics. The other day, there was a discussion of President Barack Obama's pastor on TV. Various speakers were reacting violently to each other. At the center of it was an African-American journalist who was trying to situate the discussion in the present picture of how African-Americans are living their lives together. The discussion was not about, "Should a homily be like that?" or "Should religion be mixed in with this?" The guy finally said, "Look, it is not my story. I was raised Catholic, and they don't preach like that in my church." It's a beautiful thing, an African-American reporter for CNN who is a Catholic. Can you imagine what could be done if you had that job? And I don't mean jumping up and down yelling, "Viva Jesus!" or "Long Live the pope!" You have to use intelligence to sneak in, but you would sneak in! Why doesn't it happen? Why doesn't it bear fruit like this? Again, because it doesn't penetrate the flesh.

What do you want? What are you looking for? We must live that question, because only as an answer to that question can Christ make a difference in this world. Only as an answer to that question... Wherever you find help in dealing with answering that question, follow it, for God's sake. I am not here to recruit members to anything. But the reasons I give is that I am in a context, and following a method that helps me deal with that question on a daily basis. Sometimes all I have to do is just call someone or hear from someone who is one of my brothers or sisters in this endeavor, and it begins to remind me of where I might find the power to clear the scene. Where I might find the power to face this question and know how to answer it. To try and understand what's going on. That is all. Whatever one does in life is something else. But this is where it all starts. We must minister first to ourselves, to our self; to our I. Only if it happens there in a carnal way, will it spread.

Last night at table we were discussing the case of Magdi Allam, the Egyptian editor at *Corriere della Sera* who was baptized by the pope. The point is, it happened. Everyone paid attention for a moment. What could lead a man to do something like this? I mean, not for the pope to baptize him, but for him even to become a Christian in a public way like this? In any case, his employers would like to know, so he wrote a letter to the editors of the paper. He said that he doesn't want to involve the newspaper in a very personal matter, but in any case, "Here is why I did it. Here is what happened to me." And he outlines his conversion. When I read it, I thought that it was unbelievable. This guy is describing exactly the method I have learned from the Movement. He describes the method I must follow if I want to get to that point so that I can answer that original question and cast myself into the hands of Jesus. He describes the method to help me to avoid being two things: myself and a Christian. And for us there is a problem, there is a third identity; a priest.

We switch from self to human to Christian to priest to whatever (even to monsignor). How many identities… Yet everything really is offered so that we can say with

St. Paul: "It is not I who live, but Christ who lives in me,"[2] and Christ is only one. Christ living in me, Christ, who is not myself, living in me, the risen Christ is the origin of how I see everything. I don't have two ways of thinking. I don't say, "Well, as a Christian, I hold this, but as a Congressperson (or as a whatever), I hold this...." That's two of you. Christianity has not become en-fleshed in you. You have not experienced what happened to the Virgin Mary (you see, you need the Angelus). You need to get pregnant, put it that way. It was easy for Mary, in a sense, because she could check it out. In our case, there are ways of checking it out, too. To arrive at that point, then you have arrived at faith. Faith is the recognition of the Presence of Christ. The Real Presence. The concrete and particular presence. Faith is the recognition that Christ is here, here, in this room, now. It is not a sentimental recognition, so you dance around or something. Sometimes it can be a brutal recognition. As we will see, it always turns your head around. But it is the recognition that there is only one you. "Though still in the flesh," says St. Paul, "I live the life of faith in the Son of God, who loved me and gave Himself up for me."[3] I live the life of faith, in the world. We want to arrive at that point. There is a path to follow, and I was astounded by how the column of this guy, telling his story, reveals all the steps of that path that we have been learning in our Schools of Community and meetings, etc.

---

2 Galatians 2:20
3 Galatians 2:21

On the other hand, it may be truth in advertising. At the point in which he thanks everyone who accompanied him and helped him in this step to this point, the first person he mentions is Julián Carrón and his friends in Communion and Liberation. (I knew from the picture I saw on TV that I recognized his face. I've seen him at the Meeting, even at La Thuille.) But that there was an influence, that what was going on would lead to his conversion, that I didn't know. I don't know from this letter if he was already on the path or if he was influenced to follow this path by his contacts with us, but, from whatever it was, this is the path he outlines.

First of all, it is notable that he changes his name by simply adding the word "Christian" to it (Cristiano). He keeps his name, but his middle name is Christian. And choosing that name—not only changing it, but choosing that one—is about as elementary as it gets. Embracing that freely as a name, at the very least, is a proclamation that there is no dualism in him as a Christian, or as himself; at least as a goal in his life. It's something that has to be maintained every day. But at least he is aware that he has got to get to the point, so that everyone of us would understand very well, or at least in some way, that we too should change our name to Christian. He's done it in a literal sense. Remember, we are trying to figure out how to answer that question. Whatever we are looking for, it occurs at the level of identity; at the level where I say: "I." It is when you say, "I," present in the "I" is the entire Body of Christ, and indeed the Trinitarian God, and everything. In that "I," it is the whole constituent of who you are, so that any kind of action that gets you out of that unity in the one body is a disfiguration of who you are. Again, this is in peril every moment. Once we arrive at it, we don't just stay put, not until the final construction of the One Body of Christ. But, when we arrive at what is possible on this earth, we need to be sustained in it, because, as I say, within minutes of an experience of it, it is bound to weaken, unless we are helped. But, at the very least, it's a matter of the self.

The second point here: he insists that this change in him was brought about by a historical fact. You may wonder what's the point. The point is he is saying, "I did not arrive at this point, I did not work myself to this point theoretically." Somehow or other, going from what he believed before, whether he was a believing Muslim or a secularist, he went to here:

"Now I realized there has to be a transcendence. Then I looked around to see which of the religions has the most attractive transcendence, and I found Christianity. Then in Christianity I realized that I had another choice to make, because there are all kinds of divisions within Christianity, and I kind of liked the Catholic one, because I have a few friends who are Catholic, and they are great guys, why not live it out with them, so my thinking evolved, and now I have become a Catholic."

He says it was "not a natural progression of my thinking." What has brought this change is a historical fact; something that has happened. So, if this historical

119

occurrence did not happen, something that he did not manufacture, he would not be where he is now as he understands it. That is an amazing thing to say.

This fact he describes with two words (this is the third point): exceptional and unforgettable. Exceptional, first. Father Giussani insists on this, as he outlines the path. It becomes true for you, like John and Andrew (always the prime example). You can see this throughout the Gospel again and again and again. Look at the conversion stories in the Gospels of those who decide to follow Christ. You will find out that they will tell you exactly what this guy says. It was not a development in their thinking. It was not because they appreciated His values, or His philosophy of life, His spirituality, or His message. You must understand that if there is anything that these people have in common, it is that they don't understand anything that He was saying. It's going to take Pentecost to awaken the Apostles. Not even the Resurrection gets them to it: "Is it now you are going to establish a kingdom?" Oh, take me back to the tomb! It was a mistake! The first creed from the first pope is not exactly the 12 article Creed of Nicaea-Constantinople. It is simply: "Are we leaving You? No. We simply have no other place to go. You alone have the words of life." Lovely. "We don't understand anything, this heavenly bread, and I don't know whether You want us to be cannibals or not, to eat flesh and drink blood...." They follow because there is something exceptional. This man is different from anybody else we have ever known or imagined. It isn't just because you have a limited range of knowledge of people. It's exceptional because you cannot even imagine that a human being could be like that. Like what? I don't know, that attractive. Something happens within me so that I want to say, as John and Andrew said, "We've got to be with You." Being exceptional is a matter of correspondence, as Father Giussani explains. He uses that word to mean: "it corresponds with what is in your heart." What is in your heart; that which you are trying to find out. Because the fundamental needs of our heart are given to us. It is the same for all of us. A fundamental need could be a happiness that doesn't end, a beauty that is not marred, a justice that is not discriminatory, a life that endures, that grows in intensity, rather than in the opposite direction. Those desires are given to us. They are there, the desires are there, and there is nothing wrong with that. In order to penetrate you, it has to go through those desires. To the degree that this reality and you can begin to be in communion, that degree is how much the fundamental desires are reached by it. This is extremely important. They are not developed by any of us. They are there.

These people see Christ and immediately it occurs. There is something about that man, whose mere presence, actually, whose look can touch their original heart. This is very big in Scripture and another favorite term of Father Giussani who often referred to the Gaze, or the look of Jesus. These people feel looked at in a way that they have never felt looked at before; in its depth and profundity, that is, touching their original heart. When that happens, the heart goes crazy and begins to leap. The heart wants to come out of the closet and try to learn a new life. The externality is that way; this kind of hit or impact with the heart. The advantage of such a thing is that when it happens, the very first person perhaps to be surprised is you. And you can begin to take a look at the old desires who were in there...who are starting to come out because of the power and the attraction of the presence of Christ. It makes them come out, and you are the first one to say, "Yes, this is what I want." Because, remember what I said yesterday, we cannot really answer those questions: "What do you want? What are you looking for?" The ability to answer those questions is already a dramatic improvement in your situation—to answer it truly, to experience it truly. Again, theoretically, I want justice, truth, etc., but theoretically. I mean, so I can fulfill what the Psalms say in my body, so I can see it even in the clouds, with that "facticity" (if that is a word), or carnality. The encounter with Christ has that effect: unforgettable, as long as it is sustained. In fact, that is the task. The task is that the encounter not be allowed to go away with the passage of time because it is not lived in a way that responds to it. Exceptional and unforgettable.

It brought about in Magdi a change which he calls "a turnaround" in his thinking with respect to the past. That is to say that he found it to be something new. And this is something important. No matter how old you are, or how many years you have been a monsignor, every time we encounter Christ, we are meant to discover, to recognize that this has happened through the experience of a newness that is amazing. A rebirth. An "O, What a Morning!" feeling. A development in your vision. You see what was not there before. You see something new. This is one of Jesus' claims: "I make all things new." No wonder every day we need to go through this, because yesterday is old stuff. Jesus has to match the present, and bring us the future. A taste of it anyway. Something new. It was a matter of newness; of a new way of looking.

All of this—and this is the fifth point—Magdi attributes to the Resurrection of Christ: Easter. But, it's interesting how he says it:

"The Resurrection of Christ reverberated in my soul and set me free from my old way of thinking and seeking the Mystery that gives meaning to life"[4]

His old religious views. Before, he was a seeker, and lived this in a certain tradition. But now the fact, the event of the Resurrection of Christ, however in him it became incarnate faith. We are not struck by remembering the past, that brings about depression, but by something that happens now. Because, if Jesus can't do now what he did to John and Andrew, to Mary Magdalene and Thomas, if He can't do that now, then Christianity is over. If I can't have the same experience that these people had, one of them being that He is here now and not just as a thought, then Christianity is over. We will have to keep it up, because what other thing can we work at? We need the job. But, essentially, it is over. *Finito.* It is either true or false. It is not a matter of good or bad. True or false comes first.

---

4 Zenit Staff; Magdi Allam Recounts His Path to Conversion; 2008; https://zenit.org/articles/magdi-allam-recounts-his-path-to-conversion/

The Resurrection of Christ, an event of the past, becomes a current event for Magdi. The event reverberates in his soul—that is, in his heart. It liberates one from the way of thinking one has developed before, whatever it may be. The Resurrection as a current event always does that; it doesn't matter whatever else we were before. He could have been an atheist, he could have been a Buddhist, he could have been a Muslim, or he could have been a Protestant. He could have been a Catholic, and not really living his reality. The Resurrection of Jesus allowed him to adhere freely to what he had experienced as possible, through the Resurrection. In addition to revealing this to me as possible, as desirable, He gives me the freedom to adhere to what Magdi calls "the authentic religion of the truth, life, and liberty."[5] Namely, the authentic relationship with the mystery we call God, that brings about the reality of truth, the reality of life, and the reality of freedom. The mystery that brings about the next point, "the discovery of the true and only God, through Jesus Christ;" "the God" (next point), "of faith and reason."

A revelation of the God of faith and reason. OK, faith. I would imagine God has something to do with faith. I'm glad reason is there, because, you see, what is reason? Reason is the capacity of my heart to grasp some sense to life, some meaning to life. Reason is the capacity to realize that the whole thing is not some

---

5 Zenit Staff; Magdi Allam Recounts His Path to Conversion; 2008; https://zenit.org/articles/magdi-allam-recounts-his-path-to-conversion/

huge, accidental joke. Everything, as well as my own little existence, is in it. Reason is what I have. It is the instrument by which I can gain my freedom, if I am meant for freedom. If there is reason, there is freedom. If there is no reason, there is no freedom. Because you can't expect anything. Everything happens in an accidental way. So, God is a God of reason, and faith is tied to reason. This is not just a catechetical interest of Joseph Ratzinger. This is how we live! Reason is all I have! It is my little cell. If I have any possibility of ever fulfilling whatever is in my heart, which is yearning to come out, if I am not going to live by always crushing that desire, by compromising it, by negotiating it away, then that thing has to be reasonable. Because one of the fundamental desires of my heart is reasonableness— meaning, purpose; an experience of it. If it's not there, then it is a monstrosity. Really, the only thing you can do is find some distraction. Find something that will push those desires—among them reasonableness— deep inside, so you are bothered less that you cannot have certainty. Because reason aims at certainty about the meaning of something. Can you wake up in the morning with the conclusion that life is meaningless? Why would you get up? Why bother with anything?

There is a great short story by John Cheever.[6] It's about a young man in an Episcopalian family in suburban Connecticut, with big bucks. The young man had excellent grades, was a great athlete, attractive, the whole package. And one morning the kid won't get out

---

6 Cheever, John; The Stories of John Cheever; New York City; Vintage Books (Knopf Doubleday Publishing Group); 2000

of bed to go to school. What seems to be the problem? Maybe he's tired. No, that's not it. It happens every day, and by the second week, panic has set in, because the kid won't get up from his bed. You should see the ways they try. They bring in, of course, the minister, who fails, and the psychologist...but nothing works. The point is that the kid had lost the sense of meaning. When they ask him if he would like something to eat, he says, "Why?" To stay alive! Why? If it's motionless, then it's already dead. So you see you cannot reach that point, the moment you have no purpose. Even if it is to oppose that truth, at least it's a purpose in your life. People who say that they don't believe in *logos*, in rationality, in love—I don't understand then why they are scandalized by the sufferings and injustices in this world. The only person I found not like that is a scientist I knew from when I wrote *God at the Ritz*.[7] The scientist said that there is not too much suffering in the world. There is just what has to be. This man is at least honest.

Magdi is very precise: it is not just "because of Jesus."[8] Not just because of Christ, or just because of the Resurrection of Christ. It's not just because He had beautiful eyes, because I was not back there then; I want it now. It's through factual events, Magdi said. Factual concrete faces and places. I found the gaze of those eyes, they set me free, they

---

7 Albacete, Lorenzo; God at the Ritz: Attraction to Infinity; New York City; Crossroad Publishing Company; 2007
8 Zenit Staff; Magdi Allam Recounts His Path to Conversion; 2008; https://zenit.org/articles/magdi-allam-recounts-his-path-to-conversion/

awaken these desires, and I can see them better. I discover that God, the Mystery that I find present in Him, in Him dwells bodily the fullness of divinity. Before I can even express it, have that experience, I can see that God is the God of Reason. The Creator is the meaning—in fact, it is Christ. You develop it even further, because Christ is all in all so that God may be all in all. It's a beautiful thing, this discovery.

And finally, you go one last step to discover that this reason originates in love, and now you know the true God. Magdi calls this his arriving point, a point of certainty. It is very important to us. Certainty is possible, but we are afraid of it. We desire it badly, but we are afraid it will close our minds. I'm afraid of that. I don't want to walk around with some certainty so that I am unable to open myself to other possibilities. I'm open to consider other possibilities; to me it is reasonable. I'm open to consider other possibilities about what God is like, or revelations of God. Say whatever you want to say. My certainty is not in conflict with the dialogue of other's beliefs. I don't have to give away my Catholic faith. On the contrary, the certainty that I have is a certainty that actually moves me in the direction of embracing and recognizing the good things, wherever I may find them.

As St. Paul says: "Test everything."[9] Submit it to the test of equivalence with your heart.

---

9 1 Thessalonians 5:21

Certainty is not something to be afraid of if it is the fruit of the Resurrection of Christ. However, Magdi says that arriving at this point was a matter of a long path. This was not just some afternoon experience. This is very important. Father Giussani has said this, and Father Carrón has made a big point of emphasizing it again and again and again. To know the true God requires work. You just don't sit there overwhelmed by how beautiful the whole thing is, and say, "This is it! Yes, I accept it!" and then that's it. It's really a task, a labor, a work. To go through this process until you arrive at that certainty—which is not a closing of the mind.

Finally, it is here that Magdi thanks his friends. He does more than just thank them, he sees them as steps in his path. It was by "virtue of their witnessing and friendship," he says (and this is important), "in the context of friendship, the other becomes a witness of what he or she bears of the presence of Christ."[10] This living the path with others, in a friendship is crucial. The end point is a communion of saints, so you have to look for it in an experience of that communion on this Earth. These people are not just advisers down the line, but manifestations of the Risen Christ that brought about this reverberation of the Resurrection in my heart. That is to say, Faith transmits itself through witnessing. Faith does not transmit from information, but from witnessing. And this is the big point of the School of Community we have been reading at the present time.

---

10 Zenit Staff; Magdi Allam Recounts His Path to Conversion; 2008; https://zenit.org/articles/magdi-allam-recounts-his-path-to-conversion/

Faith is a form of knowledge, not just some sentiment. I really know reality through faith. Faith is a form of knowledge that begins and grows, not through your direct experimentation and knowledge and contact with the original thing, but through your evaluating of witnesses. This is the way. I hear an airplane pass and I don't know if that may be an enemy aircraft that may crash into this building. So, every time I hear an airplane I panic. That would not be reasonable. Once it happened. But you cannot be expecting every single plane to do that. There are a lot of people making sure that it doesn't happen: air traffic control, and the pilot, who is not some kid but someone experienced. I know that, and I am certain about it. You might say, "Well, no, it could be a kid." No, I am certain that this plane is being flown by a captain who has a flying permit—yet I am not there looking at it. A whole chain of witnessing is there that is credible. What I need to know is the credibility of the witness. This is how I check on the reasonableness of my faith. Is the witness a credible one? So, this is what Magdi means: these people were not just friends, but incredible witnesses to him. Finally, with respect to the future, Magdi claims two things. He is prepared to face it boldly, that is to say, with the certainty of faith itself. He knows what danger he is in now, like Christians of all times—special times, anyway. As the pope mentions in the encyclical, from martyrs to people like St. Francis, the certainty of the faith sustains them. And this is his last point: the test of this is his loss of fear. His loss of the fear of the consequences for the steps he has taken. This is the

129

witness of a guy just a few days ago. Although I confess that, apparently, he was influenced by our people over there, it's a good example of the path that allows us to answer the question, "What are you looking for?" The next step is to clean up that path. I hope that we not only do that, but that we travel it through these days. Again, we must test it by running it through the heart (if I can use that terminology). It's amazing; I'll be 67 years old, and when facing this, it's ridiculous. It's like these old geezers who fall in love and become silly and stupid, but cute for television interviews, dancing around. But the freshness that I experience, even now at 67, is nothing less than like the first day of my priesthood. Again, it is something that I have to struggle for every day, and I have to struggle for it to be present even when I am having a bad day. It is again my hope that, as we reflect on these things, that we are exposing ourselves to these questions and letting these things enter in and not just stay in the mind.

Lesson Two

Father Giussani says that our fundamental problem is not really at the level of intelligence. It's not that we don't understand, or that it is impossible to understand. If you want to teach something to yourself, or to others, you employ whatever educational tactics are needed in order to make people understand intellectually the propositions you are making. Concepts in science and math are important things that you need to know if you want to be a doctor or a lawyer, etc. That's an educational problem, or a problem of the intelligence. Our problem is not that. Our problem is not at the level of intelligence, our problem in at the level of attention. We don't know how to look at things. We are not attentive. In Scripture, we need to be like the servant who is attentive to a master. Dogs are attentive for signals from their master. We are also looking for signals such as "What does it mean?" We are looking for that. Most of us don't pursue it any further. Therefore, what is needed is to grasp the way of the Lord. We need to grasp what God has done, is doing for us, and how He invites us to bring about destiny, which is our salvation (presuming we want all of that). All that is needed is a kind of simplicity of heart. We just hang loose. If you cannot do it during a heated tension, you cannot see, you miss things. Look as children do, as Jesus says. The reality, "the pure of heart," as you can read in the pope's book on Jesus, "the pure of heart," is not just a moral purity as we understand purity. This "pure of heart" is a pure way of looking at things; a simplicity of heart. A concentrated simplicity. There is a transparency to *reality*. Reality really acquires reality in front of you.

It's like the great description of the Virgin Mary's look that appears in *The Diary of a Country Priest* by Bernanos. There, a cynical monsignor says one of the most beautiful things about Our Lady being "younger than sin." She belongs to the time before sin. She has not known sin. She belongs to the origin; to the original creation of humanity. Therefore, there is a simplicity in which she sees things with an amazing clarity. In fact, he says that when she looks in a river, she cannot even see her face; it doesn't reflect. Think about that for a little. There is nothing selfish in her. She sees directly to the bottom. Again, most of us have dirty minds, so we have to work to regain this.

I want to say this as we move on in the pope's encyclical letter so that we avoid looking at this in a purely intellectual way. We don't want to look at this as a lesson in the seminary followed by a test. That is very important, but that's not going to save you. We need to run these words through the heart. See, this is the method. In a certain sense, I can understand when Father Giussani said that, in many ways, he wished that there wasn't a movement called Communion and Liberation (CL), because such things lead to bad tendencies. It becomes institutionalized, and becomes an end in itself. That which should be a love for what has happened to us becomes a desire to recruit. Father Giussani said that many times.

What is being proposed here is for everyone. If I say that there is a method that has to be followed, I recognize that that is the case for everyone. What does that have to do with CL? I am very grateful that I have found a group of people that are walking the same path. They are trying to follow the same method that I would have to follow because there is no other. The only way out of this is to be saved by Jesus. We cannot save ourselves. So, therefore, I have to find out how God offers this salvation. How do I even find that out? Because something happens to me that, for a moment, and it's as simple as that. Something happens that allows me to glimpse the possibility of being saved. The possibility of being able to look at things like the Virgin Mary saw things. Suddenly I look at these mountains and I see something that was there all along. First, it's at myself. That is what it means to be saved. Original Sin, yes, but all of this is oriented to being saved. Everything is oriented to this change in my life, so that I can say, "Christ is my life" and mean it literally.

Immediately what I have to do is follow the trail. I keep going back to what occurred and try to understand it better. I try to see if something of it remains, or if it is somehow refreshed. Look at the evidence. Submit the evidence to a critical analysis. In fact, Father Giussani says that any process of true education is critical. You must test it. You can't just swallow it. When Father Giussani went to teach, he said that he was not there to convince his students that what he said was true. He was there to tell them that it was true, and to show them the way to verify it for themselves. Because, if you don't verify it for yourself, then nothing has happened. If you do not think it is possible on this Earth to have the same experience as John and Andrew, then what can we give to others? Is it possible to have the same experience as the Samaritan Woman? As Nicodemus, as Zacchaeus, or as the Man Born Blind? Today, in 2008—you, a priest for years—can you suddenly have the freshness of the same experience? If that is not possible, then what can we give to other people?

It's a critical process, so that everything that is proposed is filtered through the testing mechanism. And what is the testing mechanism? The desires of the heart. And when they coincide, when they correspond, Fr. Giussani calls it the impossible correspondence. You say: "Oh my God! I never thought this was possible at my age!" Beauty, late have I found thee! What are these people talking about, and why should they be allowed to have a little kick? Every follower of Christ is called to the same. I want what he has. Where else can we go? Suddenly, you find yourself saying what Peter says. But I wasn't quoting him. Right now, I wasn't quoting Peter, I hadn't thought of him. It came out of my heart. If that's not possible, then what can I do? Can I go someplace else? Tell me please! This is why it is so crucial that we are not reading a theologian, or a founder of a movement. We are guided by the story of a man's conversion. "This is what happened to me." Well, if this happened to him, then, "How about me, Jesus?!" When have I had the experience of having found the God of Faith and Reason? Of having the resurrection of Jesus reverberate in my heart? His words! These words are not the words of St. Augustine, or any saint. Well, if it happened to him, why can't it happen to me? We have to have that experience in order to arrive at a judgment. Because experience is a judgment: "This is so." In order to arrive at a judgment, we have to follow a path, a method. This is how God has made us.

We began with the question: "What are you looking for?" This question evokes everything. It is the guiding question of the method. It is a matter of learning how to explore the evidence that will allow us to answer the question, "What am I looking for? What does my heart desire?" I mean, not what does my heart desire at this moment—that it desires a new laptop, that's fine, but move deeper. If Christ is true, then at the end of this processes, I am going to arrive at a situation in which I will be forced by evidence to say: "I can no longer live in a world without Christ." I remember, there is a set of prayers, written by Karl Rahner, on the *Seven Last Words*.[11] If you find it buy it. Each meditation is addressed to Christ Himself. Awesome. I use it every Good Friday. In the first one, he sets up the scene: "Father, forgive them...," Jesus, Your hour has come, that which You have been preparing for, etc... So he sets the scene. Then he says, "Your feet will never rest on this Earth again." He is now elevated on the Cross. Listen, when I read that I panicked. I can't explain to you the effect it had on me. It was the most horrible thing I ever heard. To live in a planet where Jesus has not stood, or is not standing, is not there.... I thought of that when people dear to me died, and I saw their feet and thought, "Never again will that person stand on this Earth." Well, it is difficult enough to continue living when someone dear to you will step no longer on this Earth. But, Jesus? Can you live in the place where His steps are no longer there? And then I realized, it's not that I would lack something, it's that I wouldn't live. I wouldn't be alive. I wouldn't exist. I don't even

---

11 Karl Rahner; Watch and Pray with Me: The Seven Last Words; New York City,
Scribner; 1977

know what monstrosity would be there in place of me. I would vanish. I cease to be. I cannot even imagine. I am not talking as if I am a saint. I don't go around thinking about Christ's feet. It happens with people you love, when they die. We get over it. We have to move on but, they are no longer on this planet. We can go all over and not find them. Christ's absence then, is unimaginable. But when you reach this point, in those moments—and it can be for only 5 minutes a year—you have reached the end of dualism. You have tasted two things: salvation and redemption. And you have experienced the desire to want more of it, and more of it. How did this happen to me? What do you do? If you are drinking a Mojito, and you're having a great time and you're thinking, "Man, this is great stuff!" How do you get more of it? What do you do? You say, "Well now, I'll get a Cuba Libre." No! You say bring me another Mojito! You stay loyal to the way it came to you. It would be immoral and stupid otherwise! What is required is obedience; loyalty to the method through which you were consigned to Christ. That's not an original passage, that's in St. Paul's Letter to the Romans![12] The very phrase. Faith is obedience to the type, (or form), of teaching through which we were consigned to Christ. Ratzinger talked about what consigned means: sold to Him as a slave. You stay. Can this dualism be overcome? Yes, but the point is it doesn't make any sense to try to prove it theoretically. It is what we give, when we get down there to preach, etc. We have been asked to pass on what we received from

---

12 Romans 16:26

the treasure banks of the Church. Treasure of what? Well, classically: Indulgences, Merit, and Grace. What do these words mean? Well, I can tell you how it is understood in a theological school, but it could be years of that. What do these words mean? The treasures of Grace; of the Church? The treasures are entrusted to us to distribute through our ministry with the Apostles. What are those treasures? Those treasures are this experience. This is what people expect of us. If we don't care about ourselves first, then how can we give it? It's a great act, I guess. We would be great performers. "Yes, but...." The moment *but* appears, dualism is rearing its ugly head. It's yes, no, or go on. There is no *but*. The method is to filter everything through your original desire. My problem is, I don't know what these original desires are. I don't know what I desire. Yesterday, it came up in the assembly, where we talked about the inner contradiction. In his encyclical, the pope is talking about that. "There is an inner contradiction in our attitude that points us to the inner contradiction in our very existence."[13] In the case of the Virgin Mary, looking at the pond where she looks at herself, that inner contradiction doesn't exist, because it is a result of the mystery that we call sin. So, she doesn't have to learn this method.

On the one hand, we do not want to die. Above all, those who love us do not want us to die. Yet on the other hand, neither do we want to continue living

---

13 Supreme Pontiff Benedict XVI, Encyclical Letter on Christian Hope, Spe Salvi, 2007
http://w2.vatican.va/content/benedict-xvi/en/encyclicals/documents/hf_ben-xvi_enc_20071130_spe-salvi.html

indefinitely. Nor was the earth created with that in view. So what do we really want? Our paradoxical attitude gives rise to a deeper question: what in fact is "life"?

Because, in a sense you can say that all life wants life. That is what defines life in a sense. It seeks to last forever. Even when life is in decline—inevitably it doesn't want to be forever declining. It's not that we want to seek to live forever in terms of calendar days, it's that we want something else that's true life, in Johannine terms. In the Bible, there are two words for it, the *biographies*, which is the biological understanding of life, and *zoi*, which is the life. *Zoi* is the happy life; the true life; the real thing. Ratzinger goes on to talk about St. Augustine and his Letter to Proba, talking about the blessed life...

We have no idea what we ultimately desire, or what we would really like. We do not know this reality at all; even in those moments when we think we can reach out and touch it, it eludes us. "We do not know what we should pray for as we ought," [St. Augustine] says, quoting Saint Paul (Rom 8:26). Yet even in not knowing our desire, we know that this reality must exist.

In this lack, in this need, in this need of the heart, there is a point that won't stop saying, "It exists. It exists. It exists." You don't know what "it" is! But your heart wants it. "There is therefore in us a certain learned ignorance (docta ignorantia), so to speak,"[14] Ratzinger

---

14 Supreme Pontiff Benedict XVI, Encyclical Letter on Christian Hope, Spe Salvi, 2007
http://w2.vatican.va/content/benedict-xvi/en/encyclicals/documents/hf_ben-xvi_enc_20071130_spe-salvi.html

writes. It is our ignorance that instructs us about this life and what we are looking for. You progress through your ignorance, you are always rejoicing in it. It's not to say that I don't know anything. That is known as stupidity. This is an ignorance that Augustine is talking about. That not knowing, advances the search of it. The more I don't know it, the more I want it. The heart is like that. Because this path follows on the way I am made.

The famous example that Father Giussani gives is that of a kid who grows up on a desert island and somehow or other remains alive. He is made in a certain way. What will satisfy that desire? He has never imagined, or even seen a woman, or another human being for that matter. What is he supposed to do about it? Where is that desire coming from? What is he supposed to do about it?

The ignorance of not knowing what he needs, yet there is a desire that shows that there is something—somewhere, that he cannot imagine—that exists to fulfill his desire. His ignorance teaches him about a reality that exists. His desire teaches him. But, properly speaking, the ignorance reflected by his desire teaches him. We do not know what we would really like; we do not know this true life. Yet we know that there must be something we do not know towards which we feel driven. This is man's essential situation. If there is a breakthrough in the encounter with Christ, suddenly you forget all that. For a brief glimpse, you taste something of It. But then it immediately ends. You will stay faithful, as best as you can, to what brought this on. And you begin to walk the path based on comparing it to the heart. Then, you run into this problem that will allow you to discover that there is a new and essential contradiction. For the first time, you will recognize how you have been wounded by Original Sin—even though you have no idea what the hell that is. Mind you, this is along the path to salvation, so that the experience of this wound is part of the path of salvation. That is why the Bible says the Holy Spirit will convict us of sin. We will recognize ourselves that way, but not out of despair. We will recognize ourselves when the Holy Spirit points out the path to our salvation; whatever the hell our sins are, original or not. Original or copycats. I don't think Zacchaeus prepared himself by a long period of fasting and praying for his sudden recognition of "what just happened." No, it was a sheer human curiosity that leads this obstinate, hard-hearted man to recognize sin. Curiosity breaks through the whole thing and awakens those original desires that try to fly out by looking for what touched them. It is possible as for a pure little person to awaken those original desires as it is for a prostitute or a tax collector. What was Jesus saying? What do these words mean to us? As they begin to follow that path they discover the recognition, "Oh my God, I didn't realize that I was this wounded." That is a gift, to recognize that. You don't despair; on the contrary. You recognize that you are on the right path. That's what Jesus says.

When Augustine is describing man's essential situation, he says it is the situation that gives rise to all of man's contradictions and hopes. This unknown "thing" is the true "hope" which drives us. At the same time the fact that it is unknown is the cause of all forms of despair. But it is also the cause of all efforts, whether positive or destructive, directed towards worldly authenticity and human authenticity.

The insight, the anthropology, the realism of these words are revealing man to man. Just as stated at the Second Vatican Council by John Paul II, GS22: "In Christ, man is reveled to man in Christ's divinity." We understand what it means to be human. This is a fantastic description. This is true. The term eternal life is intended to give a name to this known unknown. A famous phrase of the Fathers of the Church is that eternal life is the known unknown. Inevitably it is an inadequate term that creates confusion. Eternal life. This term is in the Bible, but it is inadequate, because it creates confusion.

Eternity is not an unending succession of days in the calendar, but something more like the supreme moment of satisfaction in which totality embraces us and we embrace totality. This we can only attempt. It would be like plunging into an ocean of infinite love. Like a moment which time when the before and after no longer exists. We can only attempt to grasp the idea that such a moment is life in the full sense. Such a moment is like plunging ever anew into the vastness of being, in which we are simply overwhelmed with joy. This is how Jesus expresses it in Saint John's Gospel: "I will see you again and your hearts will rejoice, and no one will take your joy from you" (16:22). We must think along these lines if we want to understand the object of Christian hope. We must think along these lines if we want to understand what it is that our faith, our being with Christ, leads us to expect.

This is good stuff. I recommend that you read it. The pope says in the beginning it is Salvation. Redemption. That's what it is. However else you express it, correctly, theologically, or in terms of human reality, it is this experience. That is why the pope says at the beginning of the encyclical that, "Redemption is offered to us in the sense that we have been given hope, trustworthy hope, by virtue of which we can face our present."[15] Those are strong words. When you get up in the morning, it is the only time you have a religious insight in terms of your heart. Even before you go to the bathroom, and you think, "I can't face today." Sometimes it is not subjective at all. "Today's the last day before they take away my house. So today, I cannot bear to face this day." How many people experience this again and again and again? Maybe not as dramatic as loosing a house. Redemption is the ability to face anything. "Oh, if I only had the power to face this day!" That means, if only I had the power to be redeemed, to be saved. If it doesn't mean that, then what the hell does it mean? Why do we even want redemption, if we can't relate it to something like these daily challenges? It's all in the afterlife. Well then, I suppose that would be it. If you can't move anymore, how will you negotiate with life? I understand an inherent contradiction in the step along the path to

---

15 Supreme Pontiff Benedict XVI, Encyclical Letter on Christian Hope, Spe Salvi, 2007
http://w2.vatican.va/content/benedict-xvi/en/encyclicals/documents/hf_ben-xvi_enc_20071130_spe-salvi.html

Christ our Hope. If I understand that, I will grasp that I am ultimately powerless. I cannot keep myself alive, that is the ultimate truth. No wonder Lent used to begin with the phrase that remember you are dust and to dust you shall return. I used to find it kind of depressing, but it isn't. It is an invitation to walk the path of salvation. To be aware of this absolute contingency is already a step along that path. I cannot "think" myself out of any situation that threatens my existence. Redemption is the sudden conviction that I can face anything, because there is something in me that is called to be stronger, even stronger than death itself. How do you know it? Isn't it just another dream, an illusion? No, it is a reasonable judgment. Why? I base it on the evidence. What evidence? All right—let's go on talking— you base it on the evidence. Tell me the evidence.

It's like the young man I meet in Sacramento. I keep telling this story. In Sacramento, in that diocese, the bishop's office is in a cemetery. What is the reason? Is it true that these are people waiting to see the bishop? That is what I heard. In the middle of that cemetery a young man, presented as a leading catechist in the diocese, wanted to speak with me. So we went outside to the cemetery. He said that he had a problem, he wasn't sure if he believed in the resurrection of Christ. And I said, "Well what do you mean you are not sure?" He said, "Well, I don't really understand." I said, "Well, he died and then he stopped being dead. Do you understand it that way?" "Well, it's a little difficult," he said. "Ok, let's take it part by part. Dead: take a look around. All the people, who you don't even see

143

because they are underground, they all suffer from the same problem - an abysmal inability to be interested in anything. They are not afraid, they are not happy, they're not anything." I pointed at a gravestone of a man named James. They had put in quotes, "Jimmy." "Jimmy hasn't been there that long, so there's maybe something that reminds you of the old Jimmy if you open the grave. But suppose Jimmy was terrified of snakes. Throw in some real wild and crazy snakes and see if Jimmy moves. Suppose he was attracted by scantily clad women, or men for that matter. Throw some in. He doesn't care anymore. That is known as death - a total lack of interest. Jesus was like that. He was moved by many things, but you try to get him interested in anything after he was dead on the cross, forget it. So he was put underground like this guy. Have you understood that part?" And he said yes, (he was kind of laughing). But the Resurrection, that was the hard part. "Well, let's say it this way: He got back his interests. I don't know much more than that. I don't know what the risen life is like, but you could converse with him as before. You could even eat and drink with him as before. That's all." And he said to me, with tears in his eyes, "Father, if that is true then everything is changed."

The evidence is precisely this change. Your judgment changes based on the fact that you can see in a way you could not see before. I don't mean little pious things, or being able to appreciate better the beauty of flowers. I mean that you see how the impact of reality immediately shows itself as a symbol of something behind it. The evidence. You talk to me about the Resurrection. Let's look at that. Let's put a video camera at the tomb. Saturday night: tomb closed. 1 a.m. 2 a.m. 3 a.m. 4 a.m. All the time the rock is there over the tomb. At one point something happens. Nothing is recorded on my video camera. One frame the rock is there, and the next frame it's gone. That's it. The tomb is open. Again, and again, those weird resurrection accounts are recorded. Was it is Jerusalem? Was it in Galilee? I don't know, I was out of town in Corinth. However you put it together, something has happened. Nobody evolved this on a meditation, or on the permanence of the words of Jesus. Something disturbed them. Something has shaken them up. In such a way that it has created something. Notice how basic it is; how elementary. Something has occurred that has created the experience and proof of a before and an after. Something before, and then something after. What is that barrier? I don't know. What is the Resurrection itself in its nature? I don't know. It's great for theological fiction, since it is an event of another world. What do I know about another world? I hardly know this one, but I know it's there. Why? Because I see it in these people. Now. Today. This is how the Resurrection reverberates in my soul. It creates in us a before and an after. A clearly defined, dated and localized, in-the-flesh, a before and an after. A change. As Father Giussani used to say, it is a change in life.

In the encyclical, in the first few pages, this *before* and *after* is discussed.[16] First, by that famous quote in Ephesians 2:12: "Your life before was without hope, and without God." A pagan may say, wait a minute! You may have problems with some of our religious views, but if it was without hope, I would have killed myself. The gods or the Great Lizard, or Zeus or whoever— they keep us going, they offer me hope. Maybe your hope is bigger, but you can't say I live without hope and without God. But, if you study the before and after, if you explore the before situation, then you will find it really was without hope. In the after, there is hope. That is the very title of the encyclical, to be *Saved in Hope*. Before, no hope; afterwards, hope. Before I had this experience, what was it like? Is it true that if I immediately eliminate Christ and His Resurrection from my life, I would be in a position in which, I have to admit, that the hope for the realization of what my life is made for is an illusion? You can test it. This is the whole idea, to test it. Try to put yourself in that situation. Granted, it is much better if you are accompanied in that investigation. It is much better if we are working together as friends. But, strictly speaking, you have the tools in your heart to do it all by yourself if you want. It will move you to seek the experience of communion and solidarity with others because, inevitably, Christ's life is a Trinitarian life. A life of a community. You can start on your own. One of the tests is that it will

---

16 Supreme Pontiff Benedict XVI, Encyclical Letter on Christian Hope, Spe Salvi, 2007
http://w2.vatican.va/content/benedict-xvi/en/encyclicals/documents/hf_ben-xvi_enc_20071130_spe-salvi.html

move you toward ecclesial life. The path takes care of itself. You have found other people willing to accompany you. But, at the beginning it is not needed.

There are ways of finding out that without Christ there is no hope. I can tell you, it is true, because this is exactly what happened to me when I read a prayer by Karl Rahner. At that time, I wasn't examining anything. I wasn't thinking about being a priest. I was reading a prayer that I had been reading since college. Suddenly, I'm reading it again, and the thing horrifies me. And I can see what he means about a world without hope and without love. And afterwards, something happens that I can have a taste of. I can taste the certainty that allows me to say, He is truly Risen (and we underline truly as the Liturgy says). Then there is hope. The resistance of this hope is itself the sign. We see as a distinguishing mark of Christians the fact that they have a future. It's as blunt as that. This is worse than saying you are a loser. To have no future is to say you are a supreme loser. The resurrection of Jesus is the proof that you are no longer a loser. Imagine life without a future. To know the true God means to receive this hope. These are almost echoes of the words of Magdi's letter. The Pope, who wants to always stun us with his knowledge of people we have never heard of, at this moment unveils Josephine Bakhita:

"I am definitively loved and whatever happens to me—I am awaited by this Love. And so, my life is good."[17]

17 Josephine Margaret Bakhita, F.D.C.C., a religious sister active in Italy after having been in a slave in Sudan. In 2000 she was declared a saint by the Catholic Church.

My life is good. That is redemption. Only the Resurrection, only a taste of it, allows you to say that with certainty. "My life is good." The encounter with the God, who in Christ has shown us his face and opened his heart be for us too, is not just informative. The encounter doesn't just tell us about God, but it is performative. It brings about an effect in you that can be pointed out. In this world. At this moment. At this time. Through this means. It is an encounter with what? It is an encounter with Jesus, and beyond Jesus. The purpose of the life of Jesus is to bring us an encounter with the living God. The Mystery, what it's all about?

This is what Jesus contributes to the world. Remember the great speech of the Pope at Aparecida in Brazil?[18] This is where he tried to answer as best he could the people's questions about why he was such an enemy of Liberation Theology. The Pope, as I know, is personally obsessed with the need to justify himself. He wanted to show that he is not just heresy hunting. He wanted the people to know that his position on Liberation Theology struck at the very point of Jesus Himself. At the beginning of the faith, the fundamental question was what exactly did Jesus bring into this world? The pope wanted to explain why Liberation Theology was a wrong answer to that question. What difference does Jesus make?

---

18 Apostolic Journey of His Holiness Benedict XVI to BRAZIL; Inaugural Session of the Fifth General Conference
of the Bishops of Latin America and the Caribbean; Conference Hall, Shrine of Aparecida; May 2007 http://w2.vatican.va/content/benedict-xvi/en/speeches/2007/may/documents/hf_ben-xvi_spe_20070513_conference-aparecida.html

If you sit around and see Christianity triumphant in Catholic countries that have as a substratum the most abject misery in the world, and if Jesus cannot change that, then what exactly does Jesus bring to the world? If faith in Jesus, Jesus through us, cannot change that, then what exactly does it bring to this world? Some kind of refuge? Opium of the people? Put all your hopes in another world? Lazarus and the Rich Man. Lazarus is in the bosom of Abraham, but the Rich Man is in Hell. There. Justice at last in the other world. But in this world, you embrace your situation in a resigned way. Come on. This is a set up for the Revolution. And so, Liberation Theology is an attempt to deal with a real situation, and to answer that question of what Jesus brings to the world. This assertion of Liberation Theology as the answer is what alarmed the pope. It was not the question that alarmed the pope. He admits that it is the same question he asks in the book, *Jesus of Nazareth*. He admits that it is the same question he asks everywhere: What exactly is Jesus all about? Why is He of any importance to this world? Can we just say that we learned enough and so set him aside and move on? Move on and keep his values? And the answer, which the pope has at the very beginning of the book, is: He brings God. Jesus makes God known. Of course, that sounds like very little. The pope admits that we don't know what it means. This is what it means: Life, a future, and all of that. That we can have the strength to live every moment as a salvific moment of life.

What is the next question in the encyclical? "Is Christianity not too individualistic?" I can just see that these questions are normal along the path. The encounter takes place without you having anything to do with it. But that doesn't mean you won't feel it. I remember someone who came to me and said, "I don't know, you said something in your homily and it made me think for a moment, but it's something that I can't explain. I just want to say thank you very much." A little gesture. You say, "Wait don't go, let's have a cup of coffee." You begin the path to helping this guy. You know it's not you. There has been an encounter; Jesus has come to this man. His heart has suddenly awakened; you are there now to try and keep it going. That it came to you is no consequence. What is important is that it came to him. And he better continue with you. This is where it starts. Now he needs to be loyal.

So, you accompany this person and suddenly they discover the contradiction that we were talking about. At one point, you will ask: How is this compatible? Has Christianity really brought this to the world? Most of the Western World and part of the East believed in the Resurrection of Jesus all the way through the Middle Ages. What kind of society was that? And today in Latin America, how come this persists? Here is an experience I have. I have an experience of abhorring what I see, the needs of the poor etc.. And there are resources, but they are in the hands of rich people, most of them who are Catholic. That's my experience. What are you going to say? He is asking you: "Is not the path you are leading me on, is it not an individual's path? Can I escape from my responsibly to give a future that is possible to a person who has no future now?" That's a valid question. Are you not afraid of it? I would say, if you follow this path you will see that, rather than make you an other-worldly, isolated individual, you are going to feel a solidarity with the smallest need of anyone. If you follow this path it will move your heart in a way, right now, that it is not moved. You will be able to offer your life for that person in need—in love—because that is their greatest need. The greatest need is to love Christ; to know Christ. The worst thing is not to know Christ, because He gives the meaning to the life that empowers you to look for solutions to these problems. Before Christianity came to the surface of this earth, before belief in the resurrection of Christ spread around and engendered cultures, there was no such thing as a hospital. It has not all been a parade of saints, but we have built hospitals and orphanages.

Synthesis

I was asked to integrate the synthesis with the Mass. But that's wrong, because that will give me the initiative to somehow or other make what I wanted to say fit the Mass, no matter what. We do that a lot. Instead, I believe very strongly that we should just allow the Word of God to say what it wants. Many times, it will coincide; many times it won't. I think we should stick to it no matter what. This time, however, I am glad to see the Word of God agrees with everything we say.

Fr. Giussani said that you cannot arrive at a certainty about Christ. By *arrive at the point*, we mean you cannot imagine yourself existing without Christ, without knowing Christ, or being in a world where He has not stood. It is not a question of having a poor existence or a happy one. It is a matter of the fact that I cannot even understand what it is to exist in such a world. Life is Christ. This is the Christian claim, and every Christian should be able to say it, starting with ourselves. You may for a moment have an insight of an experience of the Christian claim. It tends to go away rather quickly, and then we are back at dualism. Life in Christ is something that has to be experienced every day. But it can't be done unless we move, and we won't move unless we are following something.

So, Fr. Giussani says that what you follow is the authority of someone. The first authority, the first one we must follow if we want to move in this direction, will always be your heart. The Holy Father at Regensburg said basically the same thing, only using another synonym for heart, which is reason.[19] He says, very clearly, that God cannot ask you to act against reason. This would be a suicidal God. So, He cannot ask you to follow any other authority, first of all, than that of your heart. What we call reason is the heart. It is not just intellectual ability. So, the first fundamental authority, he says, is the heart. The second authority to be followed (and this surprises many people), is the

---

19 Apostolic journey of His Holiness Benedict XVI to Munchen, Altotting and Regensburg; Meeting with the representatives of Science; September 2006; http://w2.vatican.va/content/bene-dict-xvi/en/speeches/2006/september/documents/hf_ben-xvi_spe_20060912_university-regensburg.html

Liturgy. The Liturgy is the expression of the faith of the Church. And we can only reach our desires by living the faith of the Church. We must identify with the faith of the Church in the same way that we are aching to identify with the reality of Christ. The Liturgy has immense power and authority, because it is the most authoritative gesture of the Church. Everything else, such as the Magisterium, exists to make the Liturgy and the Eucharist possible. We know that from the Council:

"The Eucharist is the source and summit of the life of the Church."[20]

Everything in the Church is directed to it. So, we must follow the Liturgy of the Church. We must bring ourselves to the heart of the experience. This is the method Fr. Giussani has taught us. When you receive, filter it through your heart. When there is a correspondence, then pursue the implications of that correspondence.

These Resurrection narratives, how ever it is that they came to be put together, were, at one time, independent accounts. They are like mini-Gospels. They summarize the Faith, the Proposal, and the Christian announcement. It is great that we have this Gospel, because here we should find what we had when we began this retreat from the beginning; with the text of Magdi Allam. This is the text of a newly baptized man that we have been using to

---

20 Documents of the Second Ecumenical Council of the Vatican; Constitutions, Declarations, and Decrees; 1962-1965; http://www.vatican.va/archive/hist_councils/ii_vatican_council/index.htm

identify the steps that will bring someone who does not believe in Christ, or who knows hardly anything about Him, to an actual faith in Christ. The Resurrection narratives in the Gospel are like Magdi's story. So, I propose to you that this will give us our synthesis.

We began with these questions: "What are you looking for? What do you want?" Everything has to be played against the answer we give to that question; otherwise it will have no meaning. If it is not related to something our hearts want, it will have no impact, and no meaning. For a while, it will inspire thoughts, but it can't support or sustain anything. It has no impact on real life, and it will wither away. Whatever we do has to be filtered through the answer we give to the question, "What are you looking for?" Well, there are various forms of this question. In our reading, the equivalent of this question is the question of Jesus to these guys when they come back from a failed mission: "Children, have you caught anything to eat?" And they answered, "No." We can read this question, "Have you caught anything to eat?" at the superficial level that Jesus is really interested in getting a bite of it Himself. He likes to eat fish. Another alternative is that He cares about feeding the Apostles. Still another alternative is that this is a setup for a big miracle. This is so much more. I consider it as I believe it is, which is the equivalent of, "What do you want?" These guys are fishing. They are fisherman, and this is their work. Since they live out of their work, Christ is asking them if what they can get through their resources to sustain their life is enough? He is asking them if they have ever succeeded in finding everything that they

154

need to fulfill their hearts? Because remember, work is a crucial category of humanity—as we said yesterday—among the categories in which we are engaged as human beings. Read Genesis and see if work is not indeed the crucial category that defines humanity; to develop the resources of the earth and to live out of that. So, these characters are engaged. Their humanity and their identity is engaged in looking for life through their work—which is the way it's supposed to be. But Jesus asks them if they have found everything that way. All your desire for life, has it been met by all your work? And their answer is no. I believe that answer to be the equivalent of the first step we talked about. The recognition that what we need surpasses anything that we can ever do, define, or even imagine. Remember, we have the need, but we don't even know what it is for. For lack of a better term, we call it "Eternal Life."

Jesus then says to these guys (after having read Giussani) that they have to engage. They have to do something. Of course, I'm paraphrasing Christ as I myself was not there. He said something to the effect of, "All right, if that is truly the case, then I am telling you, do this." Engage yourselves. Don't just sit there and say, "How beautiful" or "Now I understand it!" Commit yourself. You must commit yourself to something—which, at the beginning, is almost a blind following, but not an unreasonable one. So here, that is why it is so important, and it has been the subject of our meetings. The way of reason, reasonableness, and that there is enough evidence so that we can understand, is to take a step and follow. We will not be forced. Perhaps we didn't

155

emphasize the crucial role of freedom. We can say no at any moment. What we are asked to do is to follow initially a witness, an authority, or a path. If it is reasonable, we have to follow it. Otherwise, nothing will last. This is evident from the very first moment in the Gospel. Why did so many reject Jesus? Because He didn't seem to be the equivalent of what He was suggesting He was. This is so-and-so, we know his family, what does he know? Or from the very beginning, just imagine Mary, and everyone else, amazed at who they are asked to follow, because it doesn't match their preconceptions. If you don't open yourself to that, then you will never encounter anything new. If all you follow is that which matches your preconceptions, well, then you are stuck. You are stuck in yourself. You must be prepared to follow what is radically new. There is nothing more radically new than what Jesus is offering. But again, you have the confidence that it is reasonable to do so.

In this case, the disciples follow the instructions. And in so doing, what happens? They run into something completely unexpected, and—to use the words of the text we were studying—something which is exceptional, unimaginable, and surpasses all kinds of bounds. (A real exaggeration here, because what the heck are they going to do with all those fish? Then of course, there are these little details, like there are 150-something fish!) If I was the pope, I would tell you what St. Gregory of Tours saw in that number: the age of his grandmother which he divided by 4. I don't know what he means. What I do know is that Jesus is superabundance. It is true that the Fathers of the Church went wild with this kind of stuff; they loved this material.

Anyway, what happens here is that by this event, this encounter, the disciples are struck. It is amazing! All they need to say is, "It is the Lord!" At first He is just one more item that they see: someone standing on the shore. From there, to the recognition of the Lord. My proposal to you is that it isn't exactly just the miracle itself that convinces this disciple that it is the Lord. Again, remember, the miracles of Jesus only convince certain people. It was not enough for some people to see an outrageous spectacle—not even the resurrection of Lazarus. Some people were not even convinced by the resurrection of the dead. As Jesus says in a parable, not even the resurrection from the dead will convince. There was already a predisposition of the heart. This is why the Gospel insists that it was the disciple who had this special familiarity with Christ. And his familiarity enabled him to recognize Jesus. In Jesus he detected something more the moment he experienced the origin of this exaggeration. The disciples detected something that would go beyond their wants and needs to something much more. In the words of our text, they detected something unforgettable and unimaginable.

Others are not as quick to pick it up, but the Gospel doesn't tell you when. It is interesting that it happens when someone speaks out and proposes it to the others. Now the others have to run the evidence through their hearts. And remember that their hearts have already spent time with Christ. So, it was a heart that already knew something and had a certain familiarity with Jesus. This is what began to convince the apostles that something had happened here that was outrageously and unimaginably wonderful. Suddenly, things are happening as they did before He died, but in a more amazing way. That is, they begin to recognize the Lord. Jesus appealed to the experience they had with Him, and which they had preserved in their heart of hearts.

Simon Peter was the second disciple to admit, after the Beloved Disciple, that Jesus is Lord. Then the Gospel account says (and this is what drives the Fathers crazy), he tucks in his garment because he was lightly clad. Why is that there? Maybe his pants were falling down. Mine where, as I was coming in here. (If it happens, I would say, "This is to fulfill the words of the Gospel....") But they don't know, and neither did Gregory of Nyssa or St. Augustine. They made it up, like I make it up myself. What does it mean? These guys, the author, and the editors, and the 53 redactors, are very precise people. They don't just throw in little things for nothing; there is a great economy of words. If that is in there, whoever put the line in there meant something by it, in that context in which we are reading it, and I think that is how we are meant to read it. We are meant to read it as a conversion account that arrives at the certainty of the Risen Christ. What could something like that mean? I suppose it could be enthusiasm, "It is the Lord!" He's recognized it and now he wants to go see Him, so he dresses up, so to speak, because he was too exposed. There is a kind of gesture there of preparation for the actual verification. I don't know, maybe it meant that he immediately recognized that he had to go to School of Community or something like that. There is also the parable of those guys who are picked up from the street and invited to a wedding, and the groom gets upset because they are not dressed appropriately. They could have said, "Hey, wait a minute! This is a trap!" I don't understand that parable. I've heard many explanations of it, and not one was convincing. There is something really weird about that parable. It is the same here. Is Peter thinking, "Wait, I have to dress up, He can't see my chest." Obviously, it can't be that. This is too serious; it's the Gospel, it's not a joke. I think it indicates that there is a freedom. You can always turn around. You can't be forced. You have to be prepared. You have to be prepared not to put yourself against reality; to let go of yourself. Only if this is the case can we follow. It is an interior attitude.

Fr. Giussani would use the word morality. This attitude is the origin of true morality. You must be prepared to let reality be what it is and not insist that you are the manufacturer of your reality. This has to be the case because it is one of the expressions of our freedom. There is no morality without freedom. After an encounter happens, after you hear "It is the Lord" and you recognize that this coincides with your familiarity with Him, you say, "Yes, it is Him." Then you have to continue, and you have to be loyal to what has happened. Otherwise, it will just come and go. I don't know what this meant historically, but I think it is here to indicate that before Peter came to the Risen Lord, he had to, in a sense, put himself together rather than just go running. This is the difference between pure emotion and a gesture of an adjustment to life.

Anyway, that is my interpretation, and it is as good as any other of the cool cats, because they weren't there either.

After making his adjustments, Peter jumps into the sea. Peter has this problem; he keeps jumping into the sea. (That was something which was later cured....) The other disciples at this time have recognized their Lord. It was not necessary to say anything to Him. Here He is, it worked. That should be the end of the story. What else is there to say? They begin from non-belief. It is not explicit that they did not believe, but it is clear that, again and again, that even after all the time that they had been with Jesus, they did not understand a thing about His Resurrection from the dead. So, they begin from that, and journey to the statement of faith: "It is the Lord." And it is the Lord, here and now. They have ended their journey by recognizing and embracing the Risen Christ. Now, all they have to do is to stay faithful to that, and to continue along the path. Now they have to be faithful to how they were consigned to Christ.

The Gospel doesn't end here. With John's Gospel, you have to watch out because this man (or this committee) is not out to write beautiful stories. This Gospel records very precise points. Suddenly, there is another step. Jesus feeds them. You don't need to be St. Gregory of Nyssa to immediately get the reference to the Eucharist. He breaks the bread. He feeds them. He nourishes them. It's the same story all over again. It is to say, the true conviction: identification with Christ and the final elimination of the dualism. Now you can say with St. Paul that even though in the flesh, I live by faith in the

Son of God. This conviction cannot be detached from the life of the Church, and the life of the Church cannot be detached from the celebration of the Sacraments. The celebration of the Sacraments cannot be detached from the celebration of the Eucharist. This is how Christ is to be recognized today. This is the ultimate germ of dualism killed, so that you can say those words in the Epistle to the Romans. Outside of this reality, outside of this communion, outside of this shared life, which is a concrete and visible reality, it is not possible to overcome the dualism. It is not possible to overcome except maybe for a second or two. But it will succumb to the emotions as they change. Eventually the changing emotions will triumph, so that we have to keep up an emotional high all the time. And when we keep up an emotional high all the time, you don't even see who is next to you. Then Christianity becomes otherworldly, individualistic, and self-pleasing. That experience can be had with a little drug or two. I don't need Jesus to reach that high. Jesus is not anyone's high. He is found through an objective reality of a real belonging to a community and a living of its life.

Those of us in the Communion and Liberation Movement have found a place where the life of the Church—not the life of the Movement— can be lived in an intimate way. The Church is the only communion that leads to liberation. For us, the Movement is a place where the life of the Church can be lived with concrete people, and names, and efforts, and support, and highs, and lows, and failures, and successes—just as it is in the Universal Church. Fr. Giussani says that wherever you find this possibility, if it has been a means of a non-dualistic moment, a realistic one, not simply a lie, you must follow that, whatever it is. That then allows you to say, with firm conviction, that there is no salvation through anyone else. Later, when the Holy Spirit comes upon the Church, you hear Peter say this with great conviction. Salvation is a term we talked about. Salvation is having a future, says the Holy Father in the encyclical.[21] Salvation is a life that is meaningful, and that is not a waste. Salvation is a life that has purpose, and that has value. "There is no salvation through anyone else. Nor is there any other name given to the human race by which we are to be saved."[22] And when those words come completely from the heart, we have arrived.

21 Supreme Pontiff Benedict XVI, Encyclical Letter on Christian Hope, Spe Salvi, 2007
http://w2.vatican.va/content/benedict-xvi/en/encyclicals/documents/hf_ben-xvi_enc_20071130_spe-salvi.html
22 Acts 4:12

What is Christian in Christianity?

Lecture at a Priest Retreat
2012

Lesson One

"Whoever is in Christ is a New Creation."[1] When we selected the title of the retreat, "The Priest and the New Creation," it was quite a while ago. I have to think about these things in advance. So, when I was called and asked what the title would be, I had no idea of course. I thought it presumptuous because I didn't even think I would be alive, so what's the use of working on the title and then dropping dead? But they insisted, so I said it would have something to do with God. As it turned out, it zeroed in on the priest and the new creation. Well, we can do something with that. Amazingly since then, it's not only proven itself to be adequate, but the pope has stolen the idea. If you know any lawyers who will help sue the pope for taking my material…

In a retreat for the members of Memores Domini, given by Father Giussani himself, he said that the biggest

---

1 *2 Cor 5:17*

obstacle standing in the way of tasting the fruits of the retreat is the conviction that we have heard it all before. For those of you who do not know Communion and Liberation, Memores Domini is its own association of lay people who take the three traditional vows of poverty, virginity as it's called in their lingo, and obedience. However, they continue to live and work as lay men and women. They live in community.

Every year, Father Giussani said that for him, when he did the retreat, it was like the first time. Every year the retreat always had the freshness, precisely, of Easter. Just think of it: for how long have you been celebrating Easter? And after a while, it's the same thing. It becomes something beautiful and magnificent, but it is no longer something surprising. Just think of what Mary Magdalene must have experienced on Easter morning. She had no words. There are no words to describe the risen Christ. As we will see, she had no words at all. It was something that had never been seen in the history of human kind. Eventually they die and they're not still around. But that's not what happened to Jesus. We maintain and testify to the fact that He is still around. We claim that the resurrection means that death will have no more power over Him as it says in the Bible. Do you know of any other case like that? No. There is a newness and a completely unprecedented thing happening. There is nothing like it. So, it should surprise us every time we realize on Easter, not only on Easter but really in a sense every day, that Christ is alive today. In a sense, He is even more alive than He was when Mary Magdalene walked over to the tomb, or right before His death. You have to use words like *alive*, and *risen from the dead*, but these are just words to help you account for something that is unaccountable. And yet, He stops surprising us. It becomes something that we believe, we appreciate, and we are happy about. Soon ordinary time is going to come and there goes Easter until the next year and we go back to our ordinary time. I don't like ordinary times, I like extraordinary times. And yet ordinary time is not just the title of a liturgical season, it becomes a description of what's within us. That's the problem, Father Giussani said, so he took action to make sure that the surprise and the amazement at something unprecedented would not go away. And so, I hope this week all of us, I include myself of course, will have again something of that surprise. Something that will show us, that will make us happier, and that will sustain our hope. Even though we have been priests for many years and have been through God knows how many Easters, we want to make sure that the surprise and the amazement at something unprecedented will not go away. The biggest danger, Father Giussani said, is the idea that I have heard that before, even if it is said in a positive sense. You don't have to say, "Oh, forget it. I've said it before." No, even if you say it positively the amazement can still be lost: "I have heard it before and it is very beautiful, wait until you hear it." The problem isn't that you have heard it before. We must be able to say, "I have never, never, never, coped with something of this magnitude. I still can't even begin to say that I understand it or that I have seen something like it. It is something entirely unforeseen."

165

This brings me to the first point, which is a poem by an Italian guy by the name of Montale, which was one of the favorites of Father Giussani. This poem expresses very well the thought that I have attempted to present to you.

> *Prima del Viaggio (Before the Journey)[2]*
> *by Eugenio Montale*
> *"the only hope, our only hope*
> *(and we'll see hope for a while)*
> *our only hope is something unforeseen.*
> *Something unforeseen that I have not seen before.*
> *Hope is possible only because of that unforeseen."*

But, one can ask why? How can that be? How can you say that hope is only possible when it is unforeseen? If it was unforeseen how can you hope? It seems to be a contradiction to the way things are. We hope when we can foresee something; even if it's a little amount, for example winning the lottery. We went through this lottery fever in New York and other places. I bought a ticket myself, if can you imagine. It's ridiculous because I knew very well what my chances were, which indeed proved to be the case. Therefore, when I was told I didn't win, I didn't go into big attacks of deception and say: "Oh how is this possible? I've been betrayed. I was sure. I was hoping." No, I just said, "Well what do you expect?" But yet, there was a little hope. It was a little hope because I knew what the prize was: a huge amount of money. If I had never heard of

---

2 Montale, Eugenio; Satura, 1962-1970: Poems; New York City; W. W. Norton & Company; 2000

money or millions of dollars, what would I be hoping for? It seems that hope is based on something that we have seen. And that we hope we can have one of them, or we hope it can happen to us. And we see things like that. But here this says the opposite. The Easter resurrection and this poem seem to be saying that hope can only truly be based on something we cannot even imagine. How can that be? What do we hope for? Many, many, many things. But you have to know. If you have never had this experience, then reveal yourself so that we may venerate you. You have to know that if you get what you hope for then you will be very happy. If you hope for a new car, a new assignment, a new parish, being named a Monsignor, or other such gorgeous things and you get them you will be very happy. But for how long before it becomes routine? I lease cars. I do not own one. Just recently, for example, I leased a new one and it's exciting. First of all, I don't even know how to turn the thing on. You need a degree in electronics to drive these new cars. Anyway, it smelled new and it was new. I'm beginning already to think of other things. It's beginning to be a nice new car but the word new is growing weaker, until one day when it will be just my car. And it's time to desire a new one, another one, or to want something else. So, what we hope for does satisfy us. The things we hope for, the occurrences in our lives that we hope for, all satisfy us. But only for a while. Even something as astounding as say the resurrection of Lazarus, only excite us for a short time. I'm sure Lazarus enjoyed that first week, that first year, that first decade. He might have even said, "Man, this is better than that damn tomb, they had no cable TV, and there was nothing to do." Eventually, he'd be depressed because he would want something that he doesn't get. Eventually, it would have abated, the excitement. Whereas there are certain hopes that we have that always remain, and that seem outrageous. I have told many of you of the experience I had at a lovely soiree at the house of someone in the New York intelligentsia that I had infiltrated. They don't really know what I believe. I don't want to rush into telling them because they have nice parties. Anyway, we saw a video of this author in England who was dying. The man was dying, and he could have dropped dead right during the show, but he didn't want the crew in his house. He said, "I'm going to the studio like I was in the past." I guess he kept wanting to assure himself that he was still alive. And he did. But he arrived with tubes, special chairs, and injections that they had to do during the show. All this because he would get these attacks from which he could die, but there he was! He sat there and did the one-hour show. At the end, someone said, given the likelihood or the possibility that you're not going to last long, what is your greatest hope? Is it to survive the disease somehow when every medical opinion expects you to be dead? He was not a believer but he said, "My hope, my one and only hope— if I believed in God, the one and only thing I would ask him now is for time to finish my play" [that he was working on]. First of all, I find that entirely incomprehensible. If I am in a situation like his, what the hell do I care about my play? There are so many other things you want to do: go back to Paris or something like that. All he wanted was to finish his play. That dedication to his art and creativity is admirable, I suppose. Well, at the end of the show, the announcer came on and said that the man had died last week, but he did finish his play. That was the end of the show. Everybody who was there, including these people from the New York intelligentsia, everyone was profoundly moved. So the hostess asked, "What do you think?" And one after the other said that they needed a copy of that video immediately. They wanted to show it to their children, and to their friends so they can see the strength of the human spirit and rejoice. This is a source of joy for all of us. I was stunned because I was depressed. It had depressed me profoundly. I don't want to see it again. I don't even want to think about it. But I said nothing less they think I'm from Mars or something. But the hostess asked me, publicly, "Monsignor what did you think?" Well at some point you have to confess, you have to be a witness, so I said, "I thought it was one of the most depressing things I had ever seen." And she said "What? Why?" I said, "Helen, because he's dead!" The greatest fact that has occurred, the most stunning, the clearest, and the unquestionable fact is that he's dead. The play might be a piece of crap, or maybe the greatest play ever played, but it doesn't matter. He's dead! I'm a big *I Love Lucy* fan. They show it every night and I have the entire collection. You laugh and it's amazing and they were really great but there will never be another *I Love Lucy* show. If suddenly they were to find more episodes, it would be the greatest discovery!

169

I mean, it would be amazing, but even that would become the last one. There won't be any other because they are dead. So, although the show entertains you, it can also depress you when you realize that everybody that you see on the screen, everybody, is dead. Not just Lucy and Desi and Ethel and Fred but everybody who goes in and out; even the people who are younger. They are now all dead. The last person associated with the *I Love Lucy* show, one of the writers, just died a few months ago. That's it, that's the end. No more *I Love Lucy*. I said all of this to them. I said that the truth is, the saddest thing about it is that this guy is dead. And she said, "Well what did you expect? You didn't want him to live forever." And I said, "Oh yes I did." Oh yes. "Do you want to live forever?" she asked. And I said "Yes! Of course I do!" I mean, do you want to die? I want to live forever. I want friendships that never end. I want happiness that never diminishes. I want it! But everywhere I look, I know everything is telling me that it can make me happy for a while, but it cannot fulfill that desire that you have that is somehow so outrageous. If nobody died, you wouldn't even have a new generation of people, and it would be a disaster. I guess from nature's point of view it would be a disaster. But then where does that desire come from? I don't know. I know I have it. I can track it, and I can take it from the first point of awareness that I am alive, to now. I can track this desire. I can track how it intensifies. But where to go from here to something that will really satisfy me? I can't imagine it. I can hope for it, and I can pray for it. I can beg the Lord to satisfy these desires in my heart, but I cannot imagine how that could happen. I could never imagine, say, an incarnation. I could never imagine the Cross. I could never imagine the Cross and resurrection. Never. I could never imagine that there would be a guy that looks like anybody else and lives like anybody else and maintain that he was of divine origin. Such a person, if you see one, should be put away immediately and should be treated. But in the case of Christ, there were ordinary human beings, the apostles, leaders who were not religious, and not particularly philosophically inclined as we know, who nonetheless came to believe that this man was of divine origin and who left everything for the sole consolation of being with Him. Just being with Him made them happy in a way they had never been happy before. Not just in terms of magnitude of happiness, but the way of happiness. It was a fulfilling and satisfying happiness like nothing else before. When you read the gospels in the light of that, you begin to see that this satisfaction of an outrageous desire was involved. Track down what people tried to describe about what happened to them when they were with this man. The Samaritan woman, for example, said "He knew me like no one else had ever known me," but before that when He says, "I can give you living water."[3] You have these incredible and fantastic and awesome words, Sir, give me this water! Give it to me! So that I don't have to keep coming back here again and again and again in the middle of the desert day in order to get water so that we don't die, my family, such as it was a family. Sir give me this

---

3   John 4:1-42

water. Living water: what could that have meant to this woman? What does it mean anyway? This water is lovely, in fact, and I intend to have some of it right now. Living? I mean that's weird. You talk like that, like a living steak. Living lobster, well I don't want it alive. I want it dead, so I can eat it. Unless it's sushi I suppose. Maybe that's it - maybe this woman wanted some sushi.

Living water. Anyway, they are trying to describe something unimaginable that will fulfill the real desires of their heart. Although you know that there is nothing whatsoever in nature that can do it, you keep looking for something that can. Pascal said that man exceeds himself, and that man is the animal that is more than an animal precisely because of these desires of the heart. When you have these desires, and when you can see them in the face, then you can understand the petition like "please give me this water, sir." You can understand what living water is. It satisfies that thirst. Thirst is a good word and we use it all the time. I thirst for a new companion, I thirst for a real friend, or I thirst for justice. In the thirst for justice, don't come to me with little consolations, because justice is important. Or I thirst for mercy. The director, who is the responsible for the Movement in the New York area, was recently appointed. He is a young black man named Frank who just this Easter recited by heart a poem that he wrote while in the depths of despair in jail contemplating suicide. Frank shared his experience when we had the Easter lunches together at the Memores house and he was the guest of honor. Frank was a drug addict and a drug distributor, and we really exceed Jesus in picking our leaders as you can see. You invite him to give a talk at a respectable place, but the police might take him away. Anyway, Frank wrote a poem about how he didn't believe in anything; he didn't believe in God. And yet this poem which he knows by heart to this day, a rather lengthy poem, is one continuous cry for and expression of this thirst. The poem wasn't addressed to anyone; he didn't even know what or whom or where he could satisfy his thirst. If you're a religious person you can address it to whoever represents your god, like the giant lizard or something like that. But he wasn't a religious person, so he was addressing it to the empty sky I guess, I don't know. And yet he remembers it even now. You sit there and listen to this poem and you can't believe what you're hearing. How is that possible? What is this thing in us that allows us to do something like Frank did when he was in that moment of his life? This desire for the infinite, this intense and measureless-in-magnitude desire; where does it come from? And if I have no hope, really, no hope whatsoever that it will ever be satisfied, then what must I conclude? I must conclude that life is a joke. It's cruel, and if it is cruel then the right way to live it is violence. It is to go for whatever power you can have, obtained from whatever methods you can. You need to survive in this situation; you need to become powerful. But how many can become powerful? Most are resigned, enslaved, and above all, lonely. This is a work of a god? There can be no god. The inability of nature to sustain my hope is the biggest sign that there is no god. My hope for what I hope, what I hope in my heart, cannot be sustained.

Or so it seems. This is what that Eugenio Montale guy meant when he said, "our only hope is something unforeseen." All the demands of our heart exceed what is possible by our current efforts. Man surpasses himself in desire. He is not content with himself.

There are three books that we use in the Movement to try to understand the charism of Father Giussani, but each one of us have our own story about why we would even want to be interested in the charism of Giussani anyway. Our stories vary, and everybody knows that in my case I was framed. I was set up by the present cardinal of Milan, who at that time was the bishop of some diocese just north of Rome. No, he wasn't a bishop, actually he was a theology professor at the John Paul II Institute. He arranged for me to meet Giussani and I thought he would be there. I thought it would be lovely and interesting. I was interested because he said the he learned everything from Giussani, and I knew he was a very close friend of Balthasar and de Lubac and that crowd that I liked. I knew he liked Gregory of Nyssa, which I like a lot too, and Ephraim the Syrian, and Didymus the Blind. In any case, all these guys, like Ephraim of Syria, began to use phrases that would make Cardinal Hickey go crazy, like the hearing womb of Mary. "I don't know what on earth a hearing womb is" he used to say. Anyway, mystical party people. I knew Giussani was one of them, so I thought it would be a fantastic lunch to even listen to a discussion between Giussani and Scola. But Scola didn't show up! Scola had set us both up. Giussani also thought Scola was going to be there, otherwise why would he waste his time with "monsignor what?" So, the two of us were there just together alone. By the end of the meeting when he had asked me for his help, I had to confess. I said, "Father Giussani, I have no interest in Communion and Liberation. My interest is in you. I was led to believe that you were of the type that I am. That we like the same things. I'm not interested in movements. In fact, I think that really deep down I am against them. How can I be of help to you if I think that what you are doing to the Church in the end is not helpful? And I may think just that, I'm not prepared to tell you I think that now, but I may come to that conclusion." So our stories are different. Other people would see him and fall off the horse, like Paul to Damascus. Our stories are different, but we find ourselves suddenly interested.

There are three books that we read that contain in capsule form, the "Giussanism." Those are: *The Religious Sense*[4], *At the Origin of the Christian Claim*[5], and *Why The Church?*[6] They seem to be organized in a way that I thought, and most people think, describe the path to a real appreciation of the Church.

First: *The Religious Sense*. First you have to establish, well that's say it as blunt as possible, the existence of God. With your mind you must be prepared to make sure that you are not defying reason when you

---

4 Giussani, Luigi; The Religious Sense; Montreal, Canada; McGill-Queen's University Press; 1997.
5 Giussani, Luigi; At The Origin of the Christian Claim; Montreal, Canada; McGill-Queen's University Press; 1998.
6 Giussani, Luigi; Why The Church?; Montreal, Canada; McGill-Queen's University Press; 2001.

believe in God. I was asked that when I was a scientist in the lab. I was asked how can I possibly be a good scientist Monday to Friday, Saturday even perhaps but Sunday? I turn around and I believe that the dead rise? Am I two people? I was asked that question and right then and there I didn't know how to answer it. No, I didn't feel like two people. I see no contradiction between the two, but that's my story. It seems that before you get to Christ, not to mention the Church, which is the most difficult of all, you have to establish whether there is or is not a God. The Church is difficult because Christ is in the past and the Church is staring at me every day. Before I get there, I have to establish whether there is a God, and what would be a reasonable way of figuring this out? Once that is figured out, usually one of the best cases is precisely this one about the desires. Who put those desires in our hearts? Nothing natural can satisfy them, they are even as I saw in my hostess in New York, unimaginable. To live forever? It would be a disaster in terms of nature and of the world as it is. It would be a disaster. To have perfect justice and perfect mercy? It would be a disaster. Who could have put those desires there?

Whoever put them there, that would be the person who could satisfy them. The person, or the force, or the whatever that put them there could possibly satisfy them. I could use this argument to show to someone else that it is not unreasonable to believe in something called God. Although, in Father Giussani's language he doesn't even use the word God much, he uses the word mystery. What can we say about that God?

Well I suppose you could read Vatican I.[7] In any case, after you've settled that there is a God who can fulfill your desire, then the second book continues with the Christian claim being exactly the fulfillment of those desires in and through the person of Jesus Christ. And finally, once you have established that, how do you get in touch with Christ? Your answer is the Church. So, it seems to be very logically organized like that. In an interview with the same notorious Scola we are talking about, he said that he supposed the main claim of your Movement, Monsignor, is this: and then he gave a summary of the outline I have just given you. First, the religious sense, then the Christian claim, and then the Church. And Father Giussani got all upset and he said that he was totally wrong, that he was disastrously wrong. He said that Scola was at the heart of being wrong, and that he was blocking everything. Father Giussani said that the first thing is not the religious sense. He said that the first thing is an encounter with Christ. It is from the perspective of what has happened between you and Christ that you can then read what your nature is like and write the religious sense. Father Giussani said that he did not write the religious sense so he could write about the origin, and then about the Church. Giussani said that first he had to give an account of what happens with Christ. Do you understand

---

7 Convoked by Pope Pius IX; Documents of the First Vatican Council; To define the Catholic doctrine concerning the Church of Christ; Papal Basilica of Saint Peter in the Vatican; June 29th, 1868; http://www.vatican.va/archive/hist_councils/i-vatican-council/index.htm

what he is saying? First comes the amazing thing that happens when you actually run face to face into the unimaginable; into that which exceeds totally your imagination and your expectations. It fulfills those desires and more, and you can't even grasp what that more may be. This is called an encounter. An encounter is a meeting or an event that happens, and it changes the way you see things. The encounter changes you. You fall in love with someone for the very first time. Think of something specific, some enchanted evening when you see a stranger. It may sound banal but that's the level of my theology anyway. It's a good way of expressing it because it happened to me! More than once. Except that I tried to never let her go, and she went anyway. But that's an encounter. This is not a difficult topic. First comes an encounter with Christ. We'll figure out how that can happen, but it is the strength of that encounter with Christ, the strength of that event, that allows you to see the true state of your humanity. It allows you to recognize those desires that won't go away. It is not the other way around. Awareness of the desires that won't go away is difficult without knowing Christ. Even if it was possible, you'd be stuck there facing a cold and violent world. The world doesn't lead to Christ. We just told you the desires don't lead to Christ. The road to understanding the desire leads to the need for power and the need for violence, but not the need for Christ. First must come Christ, and then comes this way of seeing the truth about your humanity. The truth is its true condition, its paradoxical condition, as we will see. And Scola, who was one of his greatest disciples, and had been converted from communism to Christianity by Giussani, still made that mistake. He talks about it even today how upset Giussani was when he realized that Scola still did not understand that everything starts with an encounter with Christ. What traditionally we call revelation is an event. It's not just information that surpasses your intellect's capacity to figure it out by itself. That information, if you wish, comes. But first comes the encounter, the event. First something that happens. Christ is something that is happening to me now, that talks about the event, an encounter and all that. I heard it myself damn it with these ears at a luncheon, Father Giussani put his hand down and said the most urgent thing is to capture the meaning and to experience the meaning of the word encounter. Faith comes from an encounter, an event. Christianity is an event. If the path is through CL, great. If the path is through the sons and daughters of the great lizard, it doesn't matter. It's where we're going. It's the fulfillment of our humanity. If the path is a charism, the gift of the spirit given to Father Giussani, then we must realize that it all depends on an appreciation, if not an understanding, of what an event and what an experience means. Because for Giussani, revelation is that. What the Magisterium of the Church calls revelation is that. An encounter, an event, or something that happens that affects you that changes your life. An event of what kind? A kind of event like running into someone or falling in love with someone. You can see the pope making that point again and again. Anyway, that religious pilgrimage of discovering, of looking at our desires and about how our paradoxical nature of wanting so much, is based on what? Because there is no evidence anywhere that what we want can be satisfied. That pilgrimage, Giussani says, ends in getting us ready to affirm the existence. Is the word "existence" correct? Let's say, the pilgrimage is getting us ready to accept the reality of an infinite mystery that surpasses anything that I knew before, or that can be known before. That's what believing in God means, and it is possible by our reason. It is possible just by a reasonable examination of our desires. You know, like right now, I am disturbed by the fact that I hear myself and all I hear is a possible theology. I love theology. I am a theologian, and although I hope not to finish my career as that, but this is not it. I am trying to make sense of my daily life, of what happens to the people I know, how I relate to the people I know, and the work I have to do. For me this is a daily struggle. I take care of my brother who has had colon cancer and who needs help all the time to move around when he can't move. I've been doing that and as a result I have stopped doing many other things. And I need to know, is that the right thing? Should I not just put him away some place? Should we both go away some place? I have to make these decisions very soon and day after day they torment me and paralyze me. However, using whatever is left of my reason, I cannot deny or stand here and say to you, "Looking at my brother and my own relationship, I conclude there is no God." My brother is tempted by that and says it frequently to my face. What do I answer? "But of course, there is a God, and you know who created you." That's the problem, you see. This is not theology. I say that we need to realize that revelation is an event. I am saying that if we don't realize it, whatever we call it damn it, unless we can relate it to something that we experienced, then the word revelation will mean nothing to you. Eventually the word Jesus himself, the reality, the person of Jesus Christ, will be a person of the past from too long ago. In 2000 years, how the world has changed, my God. Jesus Christ belonged to a world that is just not the same. It's like a banal observation, but why would I risk my life on someone who lived 2000 years ago? The present debate on contraception is hilarious because Jesus said nothing about it. He didn't say anything about war, or about nuclear weapons because these things didn't exist then. No one had set up contraception as a big deal. What the hell, these are safeguards that you try to use. Is that the one? Is that the one who rose from the dead? If he rose from the dead, then he still lives in the past. In the end, unless I grasp the revelation of who Christ is, then He still lives in the past. Unless I grasp it with my heart as a reality, as an event, as a fact, as an experience then Jesus Christ down the line will become just one more inspiring name. Just a name. A name you can switch. You can live by a moral code, based on Christian values. What are those things? They're human values. They're the values everyone has; even if no one lives by them, you at least have them. This Jesus, you keep his values, you see. There is no faster way of getting rid of Christ as a presence than concentrating on his values. Because let me tell you, there is not a single value of

181

Christ that was not already present in what we call the Old Testament. However people lived it or not, it is an insult. It is an insult to the Jews, to atheists, to volunteers, and to CNN heroes. It is an insult to reply that because we follow Christ, we have higher values of life. Jesus said himself that the greatest value is to give your life for someone; to lay down your life so that someone else may live. You think we're the only ones who do that? Was Jesus the only one to do that? We just must not read those articles in the paper. It happens all the time! What is Christian about it? What is Christian about Christianity? Seriously, we're being asked this question. We're center stage now. The world needs to know, what is Christian about Christianity? The cover of Time magazine just came out. I haven't read it, but it's written by a friend of mine, Jon Meacham. He was one of the guys at the party that night, but the cover article of time magazine this week is entitled "Rethinking Heaven." People are going back to those fundamentals. We can no longer live with the definitions of heaven that seemed to satisfy people in the past, all the way from floating clouds and little *New Yorker* cartoons (which are the greatest definitions of heaven anyone has ever made) to the great painters or to literature and Dante. These are awesome things and you can appreciate their beauty and their value, but you know that they are incompatible with the state of knowledge today. Today we know more about the cosmos, about the human body, and about our history. The definitions of heaven are not compatible. So people ask, what is the key? What is the defining reality of Christianity?

This is the question that we live and experience every day when we step out of our cocoon and many times even within it. The test, Father Giussani says, that that is occurring, is that your relations with your vocation and with other people begin to cool down. When you're all together, great things can happen. But when you're alone or with people you don't know, the enthusiasm goes down and there's a "distancing." Father Giussani uses this to mean a distancing between yourself and the other people. This is the story of every failed marriage we run into. While the children are growing up, and while we're buying the new house, there's a unity there. While we're doing things together, there's a unity of being active in pursuing the same goal. But when all of that goes away, on just an ordinary day, then you begin to get a little bored. Then suddenly in that context, in that distancing between the husband and wife, suddenly a milkman or a nice secretary appears. Excitement. Oh the excitement again! What is going to win out? Your boring fidelity or the excitement of a new adventure with someone else? Whether you are married or whether you have a vow of celibacy, surely you fall in love with people. I mean what the hell is the use of the vow if you don't fall in love? Here I have this great present for you. It is something disgusting to eat. I got it at great cost. No, this is not how you prove your friendship. You prove your friendship by giving half of your prime rib away. Here. But you almost want to grab it back. That's how you prove your friendship, when you share the other person's life. But when that's over, what are we doing together? I tell you these things. I don't even live in a parish but I hear this. I hear this from people in the Movement. I am bored with my husband. I am bored with the same humdrum day after day after day. The kids are grown up now; they don't need us. We have a financial security, we're not millionaires but we don't really need money as such. We cut down some of our lifestyle, but in any case, we'd have to cut it down because physically we're not strong. Suddenly I found that I am bored. Into that context comes a nice nurse, male or female. Who's going to win? But if Jesus is going to win, if His friendship is going to win over those other possibilities, how is he going to do it? And how do I run into whatever the hell he's doing? This is a daily problem of life, and not just interesting theological speculation.

I am not preaching, I am trying to account for something. I come to this retreat because I want to be part of it myself. And I can already hear it, "Well, it will be wonderful. Friday you will come out and you'll be satisfied." People will ask you, "How did your retreat go?" Great. Fantastic. By Saturday afternoon I will already be in a crisis. I am tired of this. We can beg this infinite mystery. I don't know how the hell you beg anything from an infinite mystery. What is an infinite mystery anyway? You can beg the infinite mystery to help you. You can even imagine the possibility that the infinite mystery has a little bit of time to come and help you. I'll put this now in the technical terms of the Magisterium; we can hope for a revelation. We can hope for it. We can even sustain the hope that it will take place. You can't have reasonable certainty, but it's not outrageous that the infinite mystery will reply. But you will have no idea of how it will take place. And you cannot complain if it doesn't happen. There is one word that captures all of this: salvation. We need salvation. That is why Montale said in his poem that the unforeseen is our only hope. He wrote that only an unforeseen entity can save us. Same thing, but now very precise. We need to be saved. When I hear the word saved, I can't help but think of the first scenes of *Wise Blood* by Flannery O'Connor. There was a lady who was sitting in front of Hazel. The lady looks at Hazel with anger, ridicule, and cruelty. Hazel says to the lady, with a Southern accent I can't imitate, "I reckon you think you've been saved." Is there a more powerful question to you, to break through to you, than that? What would you answer so that the answer comes fast before it becomes an intellectual problem? Would you say, "Yes, I was saved by the death and resurrection of Christ." That's too late. That happened too late. At the very beginning, someone looks at you like that and talks about an encounter. Someone sitting on a bus or a train or an airplane looks at you with angry eyes. Someone you've never seen before, but with disdain in his look says, "I reckon you think you've been saved." What would be your immediate reaction?

Answer that to yourself; don't give public witness now. Because the moment you already have a theological answer, it's too late. But now I know what it means. Maybe I can't explain it to you except one step further when it has already become theology, but I know what it means that I need salvation. Salvation from this life-

185

extinguishing impasse that my humanity is. That what it wants, that what it needs, cannot be found any place by its own efforts. That contradiction, I suppose, is in me. I need to be saved from it. If there is going to be any real and not ridiculously stupid hope, then I need to experience my need for salvation. If I'm going to continue to be able to tell Helen and my friends, "yes I want to live forever, yes I wanted this playwright to live forever" without being the idiot they probably thought I was, I need to experience my need for salvation. If I want to answer my friends in the lab about being one person and not two, then I need to experience my need for salvation. Otherwise, well, there's nothing.

Now, moving right along. Salvation is a powerful word but maybe I can't escape moving immediately to theology when I use that word. Maybe it's impossible for us who are priests to not move immediately to theology, especially those who have been a priest for a long period of time. Maybe we can find another word that is less technical than salvation.

Here's one: newness. Something that is truly and radically new. We have gone, remember, from unforeseen and now we have gotten to salvation. Now we're at newness. Newness is a word that moves me closer to the point I want to look at, because it doesn't introduce theological thinking, debates, or history, etc. If I don't understand newness, I have a problem. Something that's new. I want a new car. I want a new pair of glasses. I want a new friend. I know what new means. I want to say that salvation comes to us as newness. The word salvation defines a new reality. I can see how newness can keep me alive and away from the despair of the contradiction of my nature. We do it every time we take vacations. We go to new places, or a new atmosphere, just for change. There are changes that are fantastic. I used to have a gig at a church in Paris. The pastor is a friend and he had no one to take care of the parish, so he couldn't go on vacation. He asked me if I could come and take care of the parish for two weeks, so he could go on vacation. Can you imagine? Can you come to Paris and take care of my parish for two weeks? Listen, I would have killed anybody else who stood in the way.

Splendid how civilized a few funerals may be. He said he had arranged it all. It was just heaven. That change, and its effects, lasted quite a while even after I went back to my daily routine. Just by thinking about, I would relax. Newness is close to something that moves my humanity. I like that word. Salvation is a powerful word. You're drowning, and you yell out as best as you can before being drowned away: "Save me!" But maybe it's too close to despair. Newness seems to be positive all the time, except as a new obstacle. I know, then we'd call it something else. Let me move away and be precise. This newness I am looking for I need in order to not be destroyed by my own human contradiction. Why don't I call it a new creation? Now that seems to have everything in there, new creation is the origin of reality. So, maybe I can take Montale the poet, and say only a new creation can save us. Even better, maybe I can say that only a new creation can sustain our hope. Only a new creation can sustain our hope.

Now I can start thinking about what that new creation might be like. And I arrive at Easter. Exactly how the pope began his homily at the vigil mass. Easter is the feast of the new creation. So I can say: "In order to live, in order not to come to the conclusion that reality is meaningless, I need to give an answer to the question of whether God is good. I must answer that question just like C.S. Lewis did after his wife died. He said that he never doubted the existence of God, that he was too intelligent to do that. But what he began to doubt was whether God was good or not. I have to escape that situation, or to give an answer to it. Is God good? I can give an answer to whether or not there is a God; nothing is more obvious than that there is one mystery. But to whether that mystery is good? I don't know. That is not as easy. I need evidence. I need evidence of His goodness. In scripture, we are called a new creation. I like that because what I need is a new creation, damn it. The problem is within this creation. I need a new one. Only a new creation can sustain my hope. Only a new creation can save us. What might that new creation be like? I recommend at this point if you have it, that you read the second book on Jesus of Nazareth by the Holy Father.[8] Read the chapter on the resurrection which deals exactly with this problem. Let me read a little bit of it to you until closing time. Pope Benedict asks, What is the resurrection of Jesus? Do you see how this man is convinced we are at a point

---

8 Pope Benedict XVI; Jesus of Nazareth: Holy Week: From the Entrance Into Jerusalem To The Resurrection; San Francisco, CA; Ignatius Press; 1st American Edition, 2011

in which we must go back to the beginning? And in some ways, we must redefine all our theological language in terms of experiences that can be understood today. It's not difficult to do it with the cross. Like what was that famous film, so controversial? *The Passion of the Christ.*[9] What's his name, the director who was accused of antisemitism? Mel Gibson. See it's not difficult to do the passion and to do it with the power that one had. But he wanted to sneak in the resurrection at the end. The only thing he could do was show this semi-naked man pop out of a tomb, thus with the danger creating a new devotion to the divine ass. That was my biggest concern about the movie. I said oh my God! What is the resurrection of Jesus? What were these guys trying to say? That he was risen? They found no other way of saying it other than the language that was available to them. Just like we only are able to describe our deepest humanity only in the language that is available to us. This is the type of question the pope is asking again and again and again. In Miami he's getting criticized in the Miami Heralds on signed editorials. These are the official ones, but he is also mentioned in column after column. They are denouncing the pope because he went to see Castro and because he didn't start a revolution or something like that. The pope asked irrelevant questions, like what is the resurrection of Jesus? If Christ has not been raised then our preaching is in vain. You recognize St. Paul. And your faith is in vain. This is a powerful expression, *in vain.* It's

---

9 Mel Gibson, Director; The Passion of the Christ; 20th Century FOX Home Entertainment; 2004

useless! This thing we call the resurrection which we can't even grasp or explain, is not true? Everything else about our lives, especially like ethics, is false and in vain. Or maybe you have no other choice. Maybe you're too old to get another job. We've even found to be misrepresenting God because we testify that He raised Christ.[10] With these words St. Paul explains quite drastically what faith in the resurrection of Jesus Christ means for the Christian message overall: it is its very foundation. The Christian faith stands or falls with the truth of the testimony that Christ is risen from the dead. If this were taken away, it would still be possible to piece together from the Christian tradition a series of interesting ideas about God. Look, recognize what He is doing. If that did not happen, Christianity would still have a useful place in this world. The religious sense would still be valuable; it would be possible to piece together from the Christian tradition, a series of interesting ideas about God and men, about man's being, about his obligations, about the kind of religious world view. The religious sense would survive but the Christian faith itself would be dead.

"Jesus would be a failed religious leader who, despite his failure, remains great and can cause us to reflect. But He would then remain purely human and His authority would only extend only so far as his message is of interest to us. He would no longer be a criterion; the only criterion left would be our own judgment in selecting from his heritage what strikes us as helpful.

---

10 1 Corinthians

In other words, we would be alone. Our own judgment would be the highest instance. Only if Jesus is risen can anything really new have occurred that changes the world and the situation of humankind. Only if Jesus is risen has anything really new occurred in this world.[11]

Meditate about these things.

Lesson Two

The last words, the very last words, my father said to me, before he died about ten minutes later, were, "You have no shame." He was right. I mean the fact that I'm doing this, sitting here, pretending to speak to you about the Christian life; I have no shame. What we have been trying to do, in fancy terms, is to deconstruct Montale. We started with a quote from this Italian poet: "only something unforeseen." But the first problem we run into is how to translate the word "imprevisto"[12], which is the word used in Italian. The same word exists in Spanish, but unforeseen leaves something out. Although unforeseen is the official translation, if you look up in any dictionary, it is not a perfect translation. So only something unforeseen can support our hope. Put it that way. Only anything

---

11 Pope Benedict XVI; Jesus of Nazareth: Holy Week: From the Entrance Into Jerusalem To The Resurrection; San Francisco, CA; Ignatius Press; 1st American Edition edition (March 10, 2011); p. 241
12 In English, it is "unexpected"

unforeseen can make our hope reasonable. We're trying to bring it to the language we use every day. We know the experience of unreasonable hopes, like winning the mega lottery, for example. And we are saying that only something unforeseen can support real and reasonable hope. But we move to something closer by going into newness. We're slightly moving toward something we can deal with somehow to understand this point. And why do we care about what Montale thought? Because in fact, that was one of the great influences on Monsignor Giussani.

We want to understand, those of us who are his followers. We want to understand how Giussani was able to grasp the full truth about Christianity. Dostoevsky? He was not a member of the Movement. He didn't write in current times, Fyodor Dostoevsky. You know him from the Brothers Karamazov, for example. Films have been made, and theater plays. This guy asked this question: Can a cultured man really believe in the divinity of the Son of God, Jesus Christ?

Just try to imagine the type of person Dostoevsky is describing. Somebody who is intelligent and is into what is happening. Somebody who actually reads the *New York Times Book Review*. Somebody who reads that stuff. Somebody who is aware of what's going on, who watches "Morning Joe." Somebody who's with it; who is hip. Not in a disgusting way but even in an imposing way. Some professor somewhere, like Stephen Hawking, Christopher Hitchens – well they're now elsewhere, at least Chris is. Somebody like that. A cultured man. He describes him as a European of our day. Remember that the our day that he is talking about is at the beginning of the century. It's still a valid question for Europeans today. But we're not in Europe. Some of us might be European but we're not in Europe, we're in the United States. Most of us exercise our ministry here in the United States. I can testify from my own story that Father Giussani was convinced that it either works in the United States, that we can grasp in terms of our own history and situation, the heart of Christianity as he had seen it. Either it does, or the Movement is a waste of time. It will remain always some kind of Italian experience, and it will exist in the United States basically as a translation. You have all these Brooklyn kids, reading Montale for heaven's sake. They can barely read Dick and Jane. Leopardi, have you ever even heard of Leopardi? We're not cultured that way. As I told you yesterday, the cover article of Time this week is on the reinvention of heaven or the rediscovery or whatever, of heaven by Jon Meacham. I know Jon Meacham very well. I know Charlie Rose very well, and these are the type of people I have in mind. They're not proud. They're not aggressively hostile to faith, or to the Catholic Church. They admire the pope. You should hear personally Wolf Blitzer's remarks about when he met Pope Benedict. The man almost fell to the ground, as if before a burning bush. He was stunned; he was surprised at himself for having that reaction. I mean here he was, going to see someone, with some respect but with some of the cynicism that is necessary to be a good reporter today. He went with all that one thinks

193

about in those circles when you mention the Catholic Church which is basically still, and very strongly the scandal of the scandals. With the pedophilia and all of that. And yet in spite of all of that, this Jewish man went to see the pope and almost fell to the ground. When he was telling me that, I remember when Jesus asked those who came to arrest him, "Whom do you seek?"[13] and when he said, "I am He," they all fell to the ground. I mean they all went ahead and took him away. But for a moment there they were in awe. Can such a man, an American of our day, believe? As Dostoevsky asks, can a man of our day really believe? Can we really believe in the divinity of the Son of God, Jesus Christ? The question is not, does a cultured man believe? The question is can a cultured man of today, embracing the culture as it is, can he still believe, really believe, in the divinity of Jesus Christ? Now that question is on the cover of *Traces* and we hope that we can say without any hesitation, Yes! Because if we say no, then we have a problem. It's not totally unsolvable, but we have a problem, a serious problem. There are many areas in many places in which we do have this problem. Not in which people do not believe, but in which they can't believe. The Memores Domini retreats are now occurring for Advent, coinciding with the profession of the vows of new members. These vows complete the initiation process and allow members to enter fully into the Memores Domini association on the occasion of the Advent Christmas retreat. In the old days they made their vows to Father Giussani directly. Now Memores

---

13 John 18:4-5

Domini initiates make their vows to Father Julian Carrón. And this retreat, the context in which that takes place, is broadcast all over the world so that it will reach the Memores who have not been able to watch it on television, mostly because of the time differences. When it's taking place in Milan, or somewhere in Italy, it's just impossible to expect people sitting in Los Angeles, for example, to be watching it. So for the United States, we get all the tapes of the retreat. We get all the texts that were used in Italy and it is my responsibility to put it together as an American retreat. Fr. Carrón always begins by saying that the first point in this retreat is the Memores Domini people. Look at them. Look at the ones who just took these vows. This is the year 2010, and these women and these men, otherwise very normal or so they seem, are professionals with jobs of all kinds. This year we're getting someone in our house whose field of specialty, which she will practice at Columbia University, is tumors! If you have a tumor, call us. This person can figure it out! I don't know what she can do, but this is her specialty. We have people who have great specialties in the care of babies, brains, lawyers, and bus drivers. These are ordinary men and women of the United States of America who are living and working and breathing the air of the United States of America in the year 2012. They stand before the crowd and say they will never own anything again. They will never have sex and they will obey someone that they might even hate. Now what kind of behavior is that? Immediately all of my Freudian instincts appear. Why these guys and women must have had a really weird sexy childhood. I mean, that is kind of coming out now with these kinds of vows. I think like that immediately. Immediately I don't fall to the ground, but I do become cynical. It's my first reaction. Showing that I have captured inside the virus that prevents me from naturally believing in something like the divinity of the Son of God. Because the only other explanation than a psychiatric or psychological explanation, which I am tempted by, has to be that they have come into contact with something that is not of this world. This behavior is not of this world, and yet it is in the world. These are not people who run off to a cloister. These are not people who say things like "Oh, brilliant darkness," or "Oh, cold warmth!" I love it! What the hell does it mean? No, they're not out there doing that. They're fighting through Grand Central in the middle of the day. I have a friend who is a Jewish man, Robert Pollack, who is a professor of biology. He's a biologist. He began as a physicist and worked on the Manhattan project, which really began at Columbia University before it went out to New Mexico. Bob worked on that, but then switched to the field of evolutionary biology. Here is a guy who is immune from belief in almost everything he holds as true and the result of scientific inquiry. Yet you should read his book *The Faith of Biology and The Biology of Faith*.[14] He has been named and he founded, really, and so I suppose he's appointed by himself, head of the Columbia University Institute for the Study of Science and Religion. This is top notch. If you want to talk to a cultured man

14 Pollack, Robert; The Faith of Biology and the Biology of Faith: Order, Meaning, and Free Will in Modern Medical Science; New York City; Columbia University Press; 2000

of today, then go and talk with Bob Pollack. His wife is an artist; very beautiful, and a painter. It's almost from central casting; you couldn't dig out someone more representative of this kind of thing. He doesn't express things using our language, but he expresses things in a way that begins to get him out of his atheism. There are two things. Number one, a real attention to how his family was wiped out during the holocaust. He has a real attention to the nature; to the reality of evil that we are capable of. It's not something upon which he dwells on a lot. He was, however, looking at this behavior that we would call evil in terms of his biology and evolution. Does it make any sense in an evolutionary way? Are things like the holocaust reasonable, in that sometimes that's the way biology goes? People like Hitler are born that way. He thought about that. His second area of thought was what we would call, and we heard so much about today, the desires of the heart. Where are they coming from?

Biologically, we have evolved to situations in which we need something that biology cannot produce. What's going on? That doesn't sound reasonable. Caught in the middle of that dilemma, and trying to figure this out, I met him, and we became very close friends. We began to talk about all of these things. On one occasion I took him to the house of the Memores Domini of the women in Bronxville, NY. We invited him to lunch on a Sunday and he came with his wife. He was overcome. The man was there crying. Saying, "Now I know that there is a reality that exceeds what biology can do. The life of these women," he says, "is,

197

from an evolutionary point of view, impossible. Nature would never destroy itself this way." And look, I am amazed listening to him say that, because I know these women and they're a bunch of crazy nuts. Father Rich hangs out with guys who do this; I could understand the guys because I'm one of them. Father Jerry, he hangs around Memores guys too. I have nine women; nine daughters. I don't understand whether they're having a mystical experience or whether it's their period, and yet I saw what he meant. These women were far more ordinary to me than to him because he had just met them. I saw what he meant. And it was awesome. You want to cry with joy and you want to fall on the ground when you are in the presence of something that is not of this world. But it is in this world. We are all facing that question in one way or another but where we face it the most, alas I speak for myself, is within ourselves. The first pastoral field of action that has been entrusted to us is ourselves, our hearts. Because unless you can commit our heart, the message of Christianity is not credible for a cultured man of today. That's what we are trying to figure out; the core of this message.

What is the Christian claim? This year the members of the Movement will study in their School of Community the second book by Giussani, *At the Origin of the Christian Claim.* That's the perfect title because that's all there is. What is the origin of the Christian claim and is it reasonable? Can such a man as the one described here say it in a convincing way? Can it be said in such a way that would make a man like Bob Pollack fall to the ground? You see my concern is that I am saying these things and they are sounding like "Giussanisms" and "CL-isms". I don't care who's pope, OK? I got tired of having no pope during that endless time between the death of John Paul II and the new pope. The death of John Paul II had been a very personal experience for me. I was hoping for Scola; I was hoping for this. I was also hoping for the guy in Honduras, namely for people that I know from which I could get tickets to go to places and see them and that kind of thing. Maybe a little red hat, and so I thought it would be fun. But I never thought of Ratzinger because, frankly, to me he was too old. I had no problem with his thinking. He had in many ways rescued my faith with his book *Introduction to Christianity* in 1967[15]. So I was not one of those who was horrified at the mere thought of a Pope Ratzinger. On the contrary I thought it would have been a wonderful thing. But again, I didn't think it possible. But listen, at one point Mickey Mouse could have come out on that balcony and I would have been excited. Because I said we need a pope to come out on the balcony! So you can zero in and say here is Peter now. And this became not just theological convictions, but really a need. Call me when there's white smoke because I can't stand it. I don't care who is the pope. In the end it doesn't matter. What does it matter in the end who your bishop is? You can only ask these people to make sure they don't alter the doctrine of the Church. Even the formulation of a doctrine that is the result of 2000 years of the experiences of

---

15 Pope Benedict XVI; Introduction to Christianity; San Francisco, California; Ignatius Press; 2004

the weirdest craziest most fantastic people that you can imagine shouldn't be altered. People who defy every term of biology. It makes Darwin look like a little piece of shit; sorry for the language it's not my original language. I don't have built in resistance to it, it's just words. I don't speak like this in Spanish. This is true I always have to say that because some people are always scandalized and I imagine I would be if I was an English speaking person but I'm not.

So now, finally I was thinking of the man that ordained me and who died yesterday. Sometimes he was embarrassingly funny; in the mistakes he made and even in pronouncing words. His strong pronunciation of rock-n-roll, which he kept calling "rock-n-rock". Sometimes he was an embarrassment, but last night I was deeply moved. I thought about all those years ago, my god, that the man was named Archbishop of San Juan when his present successor was in 7th grade. He was faithful. He nourished us with the correct doctrine; with the real bread of life. What an achievement. Can I be sure that I would have done something like that myself? I'm sure I would not have. I would have succumbed to this or that. But there he was. That's what I needed. When we quote Pope Benedict, and I am about to, please don't ever think that we are Benedictines. It's the same of Giussani, "Giussanists", proponents of the thought of this one man as if he was the only man in the Church who got it. Not so, not so. Giussani doesn't matter; Pope Benedict doesn't matter. What matters is you. Each one of you faces this every day. You unveil it and stare at it in the face and see what you can answer.

Can you believe in the divinity of the Son of God today without leaving aside a little doubt about this or that? Can you? Can I? Father Carrón begins his retreat always this way. Look at these Memores who took their vows today, and the other ones those of you who have been Memores for 20, 30, or 40 years. I ask you now or rather you should ask yourselves would you do it again? At this point in time, knowing what you know, with all the romanticism "oh my vocation, my first house to live in community, my dear sisters you are Christ to me!" When all of that is gone, and no more illusions exist about the lifestyle in these houses, would you now do it again? Some would do it again because they are too old to do anything else. So let's get someone who can still move and get a job. Do you know what it is to get a check every month for hundreds of thousands of dollars and to give that check in its entirety to somebody you had never even heard of a week ago? Here. A friend of mine, one of the novices, wanted to buy some boots because of the damned snow and the head of the house said no, borrow some. Don't do that to me please, because there'd be no house left. And yet my friend did it, she borrowed the boots. Why would you do something like that? What is moving you? There are only two possibilities: some really maladjusted growth in your brain somehow or you have come into contact with the divinity of Jesus Christ. Blessed Marie, I think she's a saint now, of the Incarnation. You people from Canada, if there are any here, you know she's known as the Theresa of Avila of the Americas. She's known by people who know these things because she's not

201

exactly the most popular saint. Now this woman! Get a load of this story. I knew someone who is the worldwide expert on Marie of the Incarnation. She was a Bolivian mystic I knew, and you've never seen anything until you've seen Bolivian mystics. She was writing a book on Marie of the Incarnation, and she told me her story. Apparently at the tender age of 7 or 8 Marie was already in church praying; already someone who is alienating. At 7 or 8 years old I was not in church praying. Anyway, Jesus appeared or somehow or other communicated to her his instructions and asking her to take a vow of virginity. Jesus was asking her to take a vow of celibacy. To belong entirely to Him. Under ordinary circumstances Jesus would have been arrested for this kind of behavior to an 8-year-old girl. You listen to these things like Our Lady showing hell to these kids, for heaven's sake what kind of parenting is that? The money that they're going to spend in therapy to take care of him! No wonder that Francisco kid died fast. Don't worry, we'll canonize him later. Joan of Arc, what a little heat, anybody feels that. Anyway, Marie of the Incarnation felt called to belong entirely to Christ. So she started growing up, and indeed looking at the boys and everything, but she had the strength and the grace of the call. Marie was faithful to her yes until this guy enters the scene. And what happens? Jesus pops up again and she is now in her early teens. Jesus says to her, "Marry him and have children." If she were to come to get my advice I would say, yeah sure, that's a nice way. You decide to do something, and you say Jesus came about and told you to do it. But no, she was a normal, innocent girl so she married the guy. Now most of these married women who are canonized have miserable marriages. Have you noticed that? All this queen of this, queen of that. They were beaten, and it's not exactly perfect, but we need some couples that are for heaven's sakes not pathological enemies. But she was that way; her marriage had nothing wrong with it. She loved her husband and he loved her, and they lived a normal life, if such a thing exists. Enviable perhaps. Living a peaceful beautiful married life until, of course, he dropped dead and guess who pops at that moment? Jesus, and He says, "I want you now to join the Ursuline nuns. Give your child, Claude Martin, to your sister and all the money you have." Because this guy had money. I mean she had money; the successful businessman her husband had been. Jesus said to give that all away to your sister for the care and upbringing of your child. And He told her to come to the cloister. Well she did it. The sister wasn't exactly pleased. I don't mean the convent, I meant her blood sister who was suddenly stuck with this kid. Above all, the one whose cavalry began right then and there was her son Claude. Suddenly, he lost his mother. There is a temptation of cruelty here. Somewhere along the line there is a cruelty and you know what a horrible thing it is pointing towards Jesus? Well her son didn't take it very piously. He would escape every time he could and run to the convent and start screaming "mommy!" but she wouldn't open the window. Finally, the nuns got tired. They got tired of being kept up by this damned screaming kid who keeps asking for his mother. Let's send her away. So they sent her to Quebec and that is how she came to this continent, where as I tell you she is known as the Theresa of Avila. The story is not over, of course. The kid, Claude, succeeded in sneaking into the convent one last time before she left France. As the nuns were processing, entering into the chapel to pray, Claude laid down of the floor, and his mother stepped over him and said nothing. Many years pass, and the boy grows up and he becomes the Benedictine abbot of what is the famous monastery Saint-Pierre de Solesmes. And we have his letters that his abbot sent to his mother who was still in the cloister in Quebec.[16]

You should read those letters, they are awesome. They put you face to face with the imprevisto. The most favorite of mine is when he recalls the incident of her stepping over him and he asks her what it felt like? What was your experience when you did that? Tell me the heart of your experience that has kept you all these years obeying these apparitions or these messages or whatever. She said that she's an intellectual. Theresa of Avila was more emotional and crazy and mad. Marie of the Incarnation was more John of the Cross; more studious and finds more precise words. So she thought about this, what defines it. She said it was the de-powering of the soul. The removal, very surgically, precisely no doubt, or maybe even brutally, she doesn't

---

16 Martin, Claude and Marie, Mary Dunn (Translator); From Mother to Son: The Selected Letters of Marie de l'Incarnation to Claude Martin; Oxford, United Kingdom; Oxford University Press; First edition 2014

specify, of anything that is yours. The arrival at the state of radical and absolute poverty in which every ability to breathe once is already a gift. It is experienced as a gift. I read these things and this I tell you I heard from the Bolivian mystic. Either you roar with laughter and say, hey I'm going to the movies, or else it presents a challenge to me now. Of course I wouldn't have lasted a second in this situation I can assure you. I would become a Buddhist but that's too ridiculously obvious. My desire to follow Christ, my love for Christ, yes I love Jesus Christ, but would I have survived? I'm here because I love Jesus Christ. Would the love of Christ survive this kind of destructive force that wants to take away this real presence in one's natural life that is its root, its source? That question is being faced every day today. If we're going to pretend to give some kind of answer, or maybe there is no answer than some kind of witnessing, then we must face that question ourselves without fear. Only something unforeseen can save us from not being able to say yes to this question. There is nothing in this world that will prove to us the divinity of Jesus Christ as the Son of God. No, I take it back; there is nothing of this world, because what can do it is in this world. A good friend of Father Giussani in the seminary heard a lecture on the prologue of John's Gospel. After the lecture they were going up the stairs to something else, and this guy was slightly a bit ahead of Giussani. The friend turned around, and he was very excited. The lecture had been apparently fantastic, and he said to Giussani, Luigi do you realize this? The incarnation - do you realize it's a whole other world?

It's another world?!" And Giussani said, "Oh yes, but in this world." That's where the point is. A reality that is in this world but not of the world. At this point Giussani or anyone who remembers it would quote Elliot:

"A moment in time and of time; a moment not out of time but in time, in what we call history, transecting, bisecting the world of time a moment in time, but not like a moment of time - a moment in time but time was made through that moment, for without the meaning there is no time and that moment of time gave the meaning." [17]

We arrive at this point: only a new creation can save us. Because another version of Montale has saved, rather than given us hope. They're the same thing. Maybe one is a little bit clearer, but they're the same thing. If you have no hope, if hope is impossible for you, if every evidence examined completely satisfies you, then there is nothing in this world that will satisfy the desires of your heart. Nothing that you cannot live without. If you come to that conclusion, then you become hopeless. Remember when *Spe Salvi*[18] came out? I read some editorials against it that were amazing.

They suggested that once again the pope has said those who are not Christians have no hope. By the way it was quote from Saint Paul, so go and attack Saint Paul.

---

17 Eliot, T.S; The Rock: A Pageant Play; San Diego, California; Harcourt, Brace and Company (Houghton Mifflin Harcourt); First edition 1934; p. 50

18 The Supreme Pontiff Benedict XVI; Spe Salvi: Encyclical Letter On Christian Hope; 2007; http://w2.vatican.va/content/benedict-xvi/en/encyclicals/documents/hf_ben-xvi_enc_20071130_spe-salvi.html

"If in this life only we have hope in Christ, we are of all men most miserable." [19]

But yet, this is the claim: only the unforeseen can sustain our hope. Only the unforeseen can save us. So we move from hope to salvation, and then we change unforeseen to newness. Only something radically new because the new is something in this world but it's totally as something new. It is really and totally and in every aspect new; it is not of this world. And from there we move to the question of the new creation. That's where we end it.

Now only a new creation can save us. This was the Holy Father's homily at the vigil mass this year.

"Easter is the feast of the new creation. Jesus is risen and dies no more. He has opened the door to a new life." [20]

We use that expression all the time, and many times we are stuck in a rut someplace and somebody says, "you need a new life". Change parishes, change jobs, change bishops or something. Go away for a month, or feign illness, but you need to get out. People need change, or they're stuck all day long with banal crises. So we know the need for a new life. It's nothing new to be told that Jesus made possible a new life. But that's not all. The new life, the newness talked about here, is a little bit more difficult to even imagine. Difficult because he has opened the door to a new life; one that

---

19 1 Corinthians 15:19
20 His Holiness Benedict XVI; Easter Vigil Homily; Saint Peter's Basilica, Rome; Holy Saturday, 7 April 2012; http://w2.vatican.va/content/benedict-xvi/en/homilies/2012/documents/hf_ben-xvi_hom_20120407_veglia-pasquale.html

no longer knows illness and death. This new life, this newness that saves us no longer knows illness. It has no room for it, no room within it for illness. In this new life it is completely irrational to introduce the thought of illness. Of a cold, or the way to cancer, of illness, and of death. Those are completely anti new life. He has taken mankind up to God himself. The pope quotes Saint Paul, "Flesh and blood cannot enter the kingdom of God."[21] By the time Saint Paul is writing that, flesh and blood can be used in a negative way to indicate basically human weakness and propensity to sin. When used like that you could write a statement saying that flesh is incompatible with the kingdom of God; the kingdom of God being the same as that new life. For us it's safe to say that the kingdom of God is that newness we're talking about in which we couldn't even imagine what illness and death are. If that is the case, the flesh and blood already interpreted in a weak sense cannot be a part of it. Saint Paul makes that negative statement and the pope compares it with a statement made by Tertullian, "Flesh and blood cannot enter the kingdom of God." However, on the subject of Christ's resurrection, that is to say in an Easter homily, the Church Father Tertullian was bold enough to write this in the 3rd century:

"Flesh and blood, rest assured because through Christ you have gained your place in heaven and in the kingdom of God."

---

21 1 Corinthians 15:50

When Tertullian is addressing the flesh and blood, he is talking to your flesh and blood. Flesh feels hurt so it cannot enter the kingdom of God. Isn't it a fantastic thing to say this? We know our flesh and blood, just even at the level that doesn't have to do with morality. This is sheer biology. This is an eternal existence to flesh and blood; to the material dimension. Where the hell does that thought come from? And I resent it if I am told that I will survive spiritually, and that my soul will enter the kingdom of heaven. It's not enough. I used to ask my pastor, "Are there pizzas in heaven?" Just to bother him. He said no. And so I said, "Then it's not really heaven!" And he said, "That which you like in the pizza you will find in God." To that I said "Then you don't understand what's in it. I don't want it in God, I want it in Dominos." I want the pizza in a pizza that is a pizza. I don't want some kind of spiritual pizza. Am I crazy? I'm not just here figuring jokes to be funny. I'm telling you these are questions that I face. I want to know, and I am asked these questions. Every day, really. Every day. And as half of your friends begin to pass on, you begin to ask yourself where is that smile? Where are those eyes now? They have no part in the kingdom of God, but do I really want that kingdom of God? Maybe I'll settle for a little more time in the kingdom of what? But Tertullian, I like this guy. He says, "Rest assured flesh and blood, through Christ you have gained your place in heaven and in the kingdom of God." "A new dimension," says the pope, "has opened up for mankind." A new dimension of life. Remember we are not reading this because we like Pope

Benedict or because Pope X said it. We are looking at and reading this because it corresponds to answers we have been yearning for and will allow us to know; to being to rest assured. When was the last time you were rest assured of anything given the tension we live every day? You see, rest assured. This is wonderful. Why? "A new dimension has opened for mankind. Creation has become greater and broader."[22] These are fantastic words.

Easter day ushers in a new creation. That is precisely why the Church starts the liturgy of this day with the old creation so that we can understand the new one.

The beginning of the Liturgy of the Word on Easter night starts with the account of the creation of the world. Two things are particularly important here in connection with this liturgy. On the one hand, creation is presented as a whole that includes the phenomenon of time. The seven days are an image of completeness unfolding in time. What does that mean? Why should we care about it? Oh god I care about it a lot. We think more easily about flesh; about matter, about the future of matter, about space. I mean, where is heaven? If I am in the kingdom, where is that? I was accused in an inquisitorial tone by a bishop of denying that God was everywhere. First of all, I must tell you for a brief moment there, it kind of felt nice to be accused of heresy. I thought maybe they'll name it after me. "Albacetism" has reared its ugly head!

---

22 His Holiness Benedict XVI; Easter Vigil Homily; Saint Peter's Basilica, Rome; Holy Saturday, 7 April 2012; http://w2.vatican.va/content/benedict-xvi/en/homilies/2012/documents/hf_ben-xvi_hom_20120407_veglia-pasquale.html

The only heresy that denies that God is everywhere. I said, "No bishop, I am not an idiot. I have not denied that God is everywhere I have only made one point:

I don't know what that means because everybody I know and care about in my 60 years of life has been someplace. They have never been everywhere. How do you hold hands with someone who is everywhere? I can't even deal with people who are here not to mention everywhere.

So space, what is the new space? What is space in the new creation? It is part of it, it is part of it because it is part of flesh and blood and Tertullian says don't worry you have your place in the resurrection. What is risen space like? What is risen space?

We forget the other one, this is what the pope is underlying here. We forget time. Time is as constitutive of us as space: aging, being born, being a kid, a teenager, a young adult. It's part of us, the passage of time. That's part of flesh and blood. So the question immediately arises: what is risen time like? If it is true that my flesh and blood should not be envious, heaven cannot mean that I will know anymore the passage of time. You see, in the past, influenced by many philosophical views and still in some religions of the east, the passage of time is something bad.

Some of the hopes they have, their religion, the mysteries they search for, is found precisely in making yourself more and more immune to the passage of time, and hoping not to offend anyone. For me, and I'm just talking about me, I find that inhuman. I need time. I

211

hate the passage of time now. It would be fun to get stuck at 21, let's say, but not really. The passage of time is part of flesh and blood and he's saying the account of creation, that in Genesis, the first creation includes the unfolding of time. I repeat, the seven days are an image of completeness. They are an image of completeness unfolding in time. That is to say, when the creation occurs it is not complete; it will unfold as time passes and that can be seen in the concept of the seven days. What the pope is saying here is that they are ordered toward the seventh day, the day of freedom to all creatures for God and for one another. The first creation is therefore directed toward the coming together of God and his creatures. It exists, first creation, so as to open up a space for the response to God's greater glory, as an encounter between love and freedom. What the Church hears on Easter night is above all the first element of the creation account. God said, let there be light. The creation that begins symbolically through the creation of light. The sun and the moon are only created on the fourth day. The creation account calls them lights. Set by God in the heavens. In this way the account deliberately takes away the divine character that the great religions have assigned to them. No they are not gods; they are shining bodies created by the one God. But they are preceded by the light to which God's glory is reflected in the very essence of a created being. What is the creation account saying here? Light makes life possible. It makes encounter possible. Encounter. Let's underline that word and keep it aside for later use. It makes communication possible. Light, the reality of light, makes knowledge, access to reality and truth, possible. Rather than saying in the beginning God created knowledge, access to truth, communication, or encounters, it simply says he created light because light means all of these things. The others are just words; some of them anyway. But the idea is that light makes possible all these things as something we can experience. And insofar as it makes knowledge possible, it makes freedom and progress possible. On the first day, God created freedom and that's the truth. But how? Immediately you have a philosophical problem. But if you say on the first day God created light, you'll have your freedom because without light there is no freedom. It makes freedom and progress possible. If evil hides things, then light is also an expression of the good that both is and creates brightness. It is daylight that makes it possible for us to act. To say that God created light means that God created the world as a space for knowledge and truth. God created the world as a space for encounter and freedom; a space for good and for love. Matter is fundamentally and essentially good. Being itself is good. Evil does not come from God, but rather it comes into existence through denial. Evil comes into existence through a "not." It has the form of "no." God is all "yes" and creation is all "yes." Evil is all "no." I was thinking last night of teaching tactics, and I remember the story of Father Giussani when he was going to teach the notion of sin to high-school students. I forget the details of the story, but as far as I remember what Giussani did was he bought the most expensive flower arrangement that he could find. He bought the most beautiful flowers; the most artistically put together. I mean it was really a very expensive work of art and he brought it to the class and unveiled it. And even these cynical Italian teenagers had to admit that this was something really very beautiful. They would love to give it to their girlfriends, and they had a discussion about how something beautiful can attract you. And then suddenly Giussani said let's begin the class. So he went over to the thing and tore it apart. He destroyed it and threw it on the floor and said now that is called sin. This is what the pope means here. Sin is a *no*. Sin is a *no* to beauty, and a *no* to freedom. Sin is a *no* to knowledge itself; it is an embracing of a guilty ignorance. At Easter, the pope says that on the morning of the first day of the week God said once again "let there be light". That night on the Mount of Olives, the solar eclipse of Jesus' passion and death, that night of the grave has all passed. Now is the first day once again. The first day once again. Magnificent. Creation is beginning anew. Let there be light, God said, and there was light. Jesus rises from the grave. Light is stronger than death. Good is stronger than evil. Love is stronger than hate. Truth is stronger than lies. The darkness of all those previous days is driven away. The moment Jesus rises from the grave He Himself becomes God's pure light. This applies not only to Jesus, not only to the darkness of those days. With the resurrection of Jesus light itself is created anew. He draws all of us after Him into the new light of the resurrection and He conquers all darkness. He is God's new days. A new day for all and so forth. Poetry? Beautiful talk? You decide. But I cannot believe that you would be here, not one of you would be here, unless there is something in your heart that has experienced what the pope is talking about. You would not be here. It may have been long ago. It may have weakened down to who knows, barely dripping. But it's not gone because you're still here. What we need to do, all of us, every day if necessary, is to seek to retrieve it. To face again the newness that was behind it. It is a new day today not just because it is an Easter Octave. It is every day. You are created anew, older, glory to time. Maybe physically sick, glory to space. Everyday God says over each one of us "let there be light." Let us have a new light that is Christ, and we need to recapture that. It doesn't mean that you walk around every day in bliss because Jesus shines upon me. It's something else. It is a newness that keeps surprising you even when you're doing the most banal and ordinary things. Even if you're a lawyer defending a criminal in court, something keeps surprising you about yourself, and about your life. Something keeps surprising you about your destiny, and about your origin.

What I wanted to show there is the relation between the resurrection and hope. This can be seen in the words of Mary Magdalene, when she says in the hymn that her hope has been restored and has been born again. It has a very moving and adequate reflection of that. What we're doing now: we're looking, we're deconstructing, we're scanning. We are running through our experiences, and at this point Father Giussani proposes one experience – and I use the word seriously with some reservations – the word "event."

215

The new creation, the newness, the reality of Easter, the light, is all that we have used to try to understand what happened that morning. All of those put together exhibit the shape of what we would call in our language, "an event." For Father Giussani, therefore, event is a crucial category in order to understand Christianity. A category. The only one? No, there have been other categories to describe the newness of the life offered to us. Other categories to describe the new light include philosophical, Platonic, Aristotelian, and historical. The passage of history has created a newness coming to us as history passes. These are all categories of thought that can be used to better theologically appreciate the reality and reasonableness of what we're talking about; of what happened that morning, of the new creation. Already the term "new creation" itself is a category, used by Saint Paul. But for Father Giussani today, the way to express it is through the category of an event. Christianity is above all and first of all an event.

Lesson Three

Only the unforeseen can sustain our true hope. We hammered that enough to be able to say I agree, or I don't agree. There's not much more that can be said about it. We discussed that statement from every angle, applied it to every situation we can think of; every case. It led us to the experience of newness. Again, I am bothered by all this lingo. After a while, surrounded by so much talk and desire for newness, I start appreciating oldness. What is desirable about "new"? There are certain "new" things, just as there are certain "unforeseen" things that are far from satisfying my desire. It can turn out to be disgusting. There are certain "old" things, even things that supported us a long time ago that continue doing so now. So, I hesitate a bit to say that's done, let's move on. I still want to experience more, not because I am interested in linguistics, but because of what is at stake. What we're discussing is the ultimate question, not theoretically ultimate, but concerning the value of my existence, of my life. There's no more important question than that one. So therefore when I find out what I want to know, what's there in newness that increase my life and strengthens it, I'm not just asking a theoretical linguistic question. I am looking to arrive at some kind of certainty of judgment about the value of my life. Listen to any proposal. Somebody comes and tells you "its like this." I'll begin to listen and will stay listening if it continues being worthwhile. But if it is not worthwhile, then forget about it. I don't have time for speculation. I want an investigation on the goodness of the "new" in newness. It even sounds stupid. In any case, this is the proposal. There is one set of human experiences which everybody has, and which everyone is able to retrieve from within without much difficulty. There is one category of experience that will help you understand this whole question. What is there about "new" in newness? What is there about "old" in oldness? What is a new creation? What is unexpected about the whole thing; about the path we have traveled? And that is the category of event. Look for clues in your experiences of what you call "an event". Sure, again, that's one more word. Once again I am initially a little bit skeptical because this word game continues endlessly. But on the other hand I desire not to pay attention to it realizing the seriousness of the question that is involved. Especially at a certain age like the one I am where you can drop dead and no one will say "that was unforeseen." I care to find out what the heck's going to happen. Is there a more important question? So that helps me overcome the initial resistance I would by now have. You go to the toilet and it's an event. That's what it is! But let's give it a chance. Turns out the pope is into events, too. An event is simply something that happens to you. Something that touches you, that concerns you, and that awakens a concern in you. Maybe concern is the wrong word. Awakens your attention. I mean if you're taking a nap, sleeping, watching TV, reading, there are all kinds of things going on. There are noises of people talking and you don't even hear them. These things are happening, but they are not events for you because they don't awaken anything. Above all they don't awaken you to demonstrate to you something that you had not foreseen but which is of interest. We talked about going into a busy bus station, or train station, or airport. Everybody, mobs of people, are talking or running to get the train. You hear all of the incomprehensible train announcements, that kind of stuff. And your attention span is directly on board, whatever it is you're getting on board. But suddenly you hear your name. You hear it from a voice you recognize, and preferably a sweet inviting voice. You pay attention; you look for it. Remember the incident in the gospel where the woman with the hemorrhage touches Jesus. She was convinced that if she touched Him the problem would be over. Like 38 years without health insurance, and after seeing all the doctors; she did it. She touched Jesus and the whole thing disappeared. Remember Jesus' concern to look and find out who it was. And the Apostles said look there are mobs of people, forget it, come on. But Jesus won't give up; he's got his radar going looking to however the eternal son of God, incarnate of the Blessed Virgin Mary determines these things, I don't know. He was captured by the event. The event awakened him to something he had to do. It could be the other way around it could reawaken me to something I have to run away from. The important thing is that it reawakens me to something that I judge as important to me. This is what an event is. The Christian proclamation, the Christian claim, is that the truth of where we come from and why we're here is called a revelation. Where we're going, how to get there, and what it involves, all of that in classical terms is called a revelation. The proposal is that the category that best serves to make this proclamation today in light of the cultural situation we have discussed is that of an event. Better than revelation, better than history, better than philosophical categories of Hellenistic origins. There is nothing wrong with these! The Church has to proclaim the gospel at the time in which she's at. It is now that we make the Christian claim to everyone and to ourselves. It is now. The much maligned signs of the times, the concept of the Second Vatican Council, is really important even if it was misused to justify a lot of stupid silly stuff. We need to assess the situation as it is now, and that doesn't mean that these other words are not true. It simply means that it seems that the category of event is one that best captures my attention now. It allows me to propose a Christianity that might be more alive and attractive to the person to whom I am making the proclamation.

The category of event as an expression of what otherwise we would call revelation needs to be subjected to the same kind of philosophical and theological study and development as all the other categories that have been used. It hasn't been. Some of our own people, I mean CL scholars, philosophers, and theologians, are working on that now. And there are references that could be given of work done, but it is not in English, so it is not of much use. By the way, that doesn't stand in the way. I want to say that has to be done. It would be nice to have a controversy, so you would have people you admire and respect attack the category of event so that we would need to defend it. All that is fascinating. All that philosophical and theological dialogue that keeps those people off the street. I love that stuff and it's great to read. You know the dialogue between Habermas and Ratzinger a few months before Ratzinger was named pope? Habermas is a German philosopher, the father of German secularism, and he was never anti-Catholic in the sense that he was insulting the Catholic Church. However, at the beginning of his philosophical career he wouldn't even consider that Catholics might have anything interesting to say today. His task, his desire, is to show that you do not need religion and faith in order to support a worldwide ethical system. He wants to show that you do not need religion to help fight terrorism, the spread of nuclear warfare, policies against women, and all that kind of stuff. He acknowledges that secularism seems to undercut the basis of why anyone would want to behave morally. And to what do you appeal? Some regimes here in the United States have appealed to human rights. We're all upset because in China human rights are being violated. But you know the answer. The answer is what you consider human rights. Everyone has his own version of human rights; each tradition and each country.

Don't criticize us, we won't criticize you. So the notion of human rights is useless. The notion of human dignity. You hear these people. Hitler could stand and defend human dignity. Should it mean the same thing we mean by it? So it's a useless category. Habermas has been writing about this, convinced though, that secularism can generate an ethical code that will be respected and valued by everyone. There will still

221

be crime and after all we are the way we are. We sell our own grandmothers, it doesn't matter. It's not that everyone will suddenly behave better. He said it could be something like a code to which something like a world-wide international court can appeal. And for an anniversary, like you know his 400th birthday or something, some of his followers and people at the university decided to have an open discussion. So on the Catholic side they selected Joseph Ratzinger who accepted. There were moments in which Pope John Paul II was concerned that Ratzinger was accepting too many of these invitations. Like he thought he was going to screw it up; something was going to be said that shouldn't be said due to his enthusiasm and everything. The pope was concerned that Ratzinger was going to have a big problem because he would be on record. Ratzinger was suddenly a star. I mean you would go to see the theaters in Rome and they would be advertising that this coming Wednesday, a debate between Joseph Ratzinger and so and so would be broadcast. The theaters would be packed, and you would have a big screen TV outside. Can you imagine? And Ratzinger would show up, not in the glorious vestments he had access to, but like an ordinary priest. And he would sit there, mediated by some important celebrity, and on the other side would be the head of the communist thought police. Joseph Ratzinger and the other speaker would have a discussion and they would publish it in a journal of atheistic thought to which I subscribe, and it would be a big hit. You can't do it here. First of all whom would you put up against anybody? That was what they attempted with Christopher Hitchens and they invited me at the last minute. I was stupid enough to accept, and they asked me to be the Catholic representative. I thought I was being invited to a panel. I didn't know it would be just me; suddenly the bearer of the Catholic Church and of all of its hopes and claims. Suddenly I was not just the Catholic Church but the whole religious world because Hitchens was against God, against the Mystery. Here is Albacete dragging his ass over there to defend the unforeseen. If you were the unforeseen you'd take measures to correct that situation even if you have to stage an apparition. Which I expected at any moment because the last time when I went to defend the Virginity of Mary on a CNN program around Christmas time. I was defending Mary against the writings of one of the most ridiculous figures in the world, and I'm telling you in private life, he was just the same, he was the Episcopal bishop of Newark. First of all that such a monstrosity exists is unbelievable. Anyway, he fits it. And he looked really neat, and his shoes would shine. He had the best pedicure, manicures, eye cures, and everything. He was on the side that Mary was raped, because that was what his book finally concluded. On the other side, ta-da, me, defender of Mary's virtue. I didn't know what to do. I said no, there's no way, no dialogue, there's no way you can really talk about this. It's just a clash of phrases that you say, that you come armed with and drop here and there instead of a real conversation. Sound bites. These are wars of sound bites. Who's more attractive: this guy with his latex shoes or this fat monsignor? This

Episcopal Bishop says that Mary was raped, and this fat monsignor, with coffee all himself is saying, "No, no she was immaculate." Who won? So I said no, until the woman who was on the phone with me said, "I am no longer talking to you as a representative of CNN, I am speaking to you as a Christian. I am not a Catholic, but I am a Christian and I believe in the virginal conception of Jesus. I ask you please, everybody tells me no, I ask you to defend Our Lady." What are you going to say? Once more our Holy Mother is being used as spiritual blackmail against me. I think Giussani saw that call. What are you going to do? Alright, let's defend Our Lady. Let's go, what the hell. The spirit will tell you what to do. Don't worry about what you're going to do. So I said, you know what, I am not going to worry. And the day comes, and I'll show up and say, no Jesus was immaculately conceived. Without a father, whatever the heck. This idiot, nicely dressed, would never understand. What did you go out to the desert to see? I mean you could go crazy quoting things. I would be just as good quoting material. But anyway, no there was great concern. At that time I was teaching at the John Paul II Institute in Washington. There was no great concern that I would blow it up and I would get memos from scholars telling me defend this latest finding about Aramaic something or other. I was never going to read that stuff. Again, this wasn't exactly a discussion sponsored by the Harvard Divinity school. This was some stupid woman's show, come on. It's show business; it's not a theological discussion. I know what I'm going to do. I am going to go dressed up as a revolutionary liberation theologian demanding there be revolution to change all the social structures of Latin America. I will say that among the most pernicious things the United States is doing is infiltrating into Latin America's so-called religious pastors that denounce the Blessed Virgin Mary who is the one who holds us all together as sons and daughters of the same continent. This is an American plot. This guy is probably on the pay-roll of the CIA for writing his book. I would go dressed with my guayabera and machete and I did. Stopping at a little statue of Our Lady in the parish I said, "Mary this is it, here we go. Help me defend you because I look pretty stupid like this." And you know, at the last minute, right before we were about to begin, they canceled it because of some worldwide event they had to cover suddenly. Whatever it was, you could see that they do those things, they have to do that. Their big claim is to be able to interrupt whatever stupid thing they are doing to give you the latest and most urgent news. So they canceled it. I was relieved, because I didn't even really know how to hold a machete anyway. They were terrified when they saw me. They didn't expect that. I went back to the parish and I started getting angry. I went to Our Lady said that you could have shown a little greater confidence in me. You can't just kill some foreign leader somewhere in order to cancel the show so that your integrity wouldn't be in my hands. This has nothing to do with what we need to be talking about. Ratzinger and Habermas, so they had their meeting.

And that you can buy in English. *The Dialectics of Reason*,[23] I think it's called. On the cover you see Ratzinger talking with Habermas and it is a fascinating discussion. Among the things that happens, Ratzinger goes one by one over these concepts that have been used in order to try to transmit the heart of the Christian proposal. He tries to give the witness to what we have experienced and what we want to share with others. Ratzinger goes over the idea of revelation, and the idea of history, to name a few. He says that they don't hold any water today. Ratzinger agrees with Habermas that they are not convincing. The secularist thought has advanced to a point that it has a way of dealing with these things, just as secularist politics has found a way of dealing with the religious sense and faith that neutralizes the impact which this could have on social life and on politics. This gives rise to the question that if you are not in hiding in some cave you must have asked yourself,: what is the impact of the Christian faith on politics? It is a valid question. What should it be? Should it have anything to do with politics? Should there be a separation between the two? I'm not talking about the separation between church and state. That's a valid question too; it's not the relation between church and state. The real question is faith. What I believe about reality, that faith, can it impact politics? Should it have a political dimension to it so that it engages me in a particular kind of politics? Even to the point of

23 Joseph Ratzinger, Jürgen Habermas; The Dialectics of Secularization: On Reason and Religion; San Francisco, California; Ignatius Press; 2007

supporting whether I will vote for Romney or Obama? This question has begun to surface for many people. Ratzinger says that secularist thought has neutralized this category. Natural law, that's an interesting point. In the book Ratzinger says that at the present time there is no other language, no other philosophical system, with which to proclaim the gospel to nonbelievers than an appeal to the reality of a natural law. And it has to continue doing so. Until something else is found, we're going to have to be able to appeal, as fancy sounding as possible, to an alliance with creative wisdom. That's what natural law stands for. You see, in a certain sense, the battle for attention? I won't talk to you about natural law but I'm willing to talk to you about the human alliance with creative wisdom. It's exactly the same damn thing but I'll tell you, you'll pay more attention to that than to a natural law discussion. So in a sense, don't put it down to the search for a category that has the power to awaken! And Ratzinger says, the natural law category doesn't have that power anymore. It has sunk. I was surprised at the terminology he uses. At the end they can only conclude that this kind of dialogue should continue. Until something shows up, we should persist in an atmosphere of decency like what they had. Yet maybe what Ratzinger says at one point will happen. The Holy Spirit and a grace will come to propose the terminology for us that will attract us both together and we can begin to attempt to walk together. I believe in the Holy Spirit that will allow us to work together on behalf of this world which is so threatened by the lack of an ethical worldwide system. That's how it ends.

Then he ran off and became pope. You can imagine Habermas. Students of both decided to continue the dialogue and you can get a book which is the next step in the dialogue between Ratzinger and Habermas.[24] Their students went ahead and continued this kind of conversation. And Habermas wrote an essay for the new book that is fascinating because there are a lot of people discussing it. Is Habermas coming around to a next stage in his thinking? Not that he's going to come out and say kneel down and sing the Salve Regina, but is he willing to admit that a radical secularism is doomed to be fruitless? Will he admit that secularism will not generate a way of life that will support human dignity, or what? Because the title of the book and based on his essay is "What is Missing" or something is missing.

But, Giussani makes clear, this is all fascinating and we need a theological analysis of the category of "event" but that is something separate that is for theologians, for scholars etc. We need to look at it as a fact of our daily experience. It is very dangerous. Yes we have said before theology and philosophy are absolutely necessary, but very dangerous because you can seek and maybe achieve an understanding, a brilliant one that will do nothing to you. It won't change you a bit. It may sustain you with an enthusiasm and maybe a little money for the sale of your book of running into a popular philosophical or theological concept, although in theology I assure you—you will never

---

24 Habermas, Jürgen; An Awareness of What is Missing: Faith and Reason in a Post-secular Age; Cambridge, United Kingdom; Polity; 2010

make big money unless you are the Episcopal Bishop of Newark, perhaps you can write disguised as one of those, why not? Nonetheless, as important as it is, it is very dangerous, because it will reach us, it threatens to take us to a position in which we think we have understood the geniality of the Christian claim: "now I understand." Intellectually, an understanding without an understanding of the heart that moves you and changes you, we have not understood. In fact, we may be stuck into a valid and true intellectual understanding of it, that may have become an obstacle to the real existential if I may use that word, experiential understanding of it. And to that I can testify. There isn't a single thought, after I overcame the lingo problem, there wasn't a single thought that Giussani had to teach to me, that I had not already learned and was not teaching at the John Paul II Institute. In terms of theological content, I have learned very little from Giussani, but my god have I come to see the gigantic mountain of an obstacle that such knowledge had created for me, keeping me away from a real knowledge in the biblical sense including affectivity, amazement, gratitude, and a real knowledge. It's like when you fall in love, you know someone and as time passes you know more and more. What is it that makes it exciting, the more facts that you know? "Oh now I know when she had her tonsils removed."

Well, it is interesting, but it isn't exactly going to support a life together. It is all in the service of "I know her better, I know her more, she knows me this way." Do you see? Do you understand? And that second type of knowledge, which is what we really need, cannot be abandoned to the realm of unreasonable or to sentiment. If the theological form of knowledge is a rigorous scientifically-ruled norm that it must follow if you're going to take it seriously as a theologian or a philosopher today, so must the other. I don't know what to call it, "x?" The use of the category of event must also be subjected to a rigorous scientifically-ruled norm. Perhaps it would be very good to have a skeptical response to it. No, come on, the only reason suddenly that you say you understand is because you are older and you older people understand certain things better. This is what is happening to you. You begin to change, and wait a minute! Under the influence of a show like Rimini and now the New York Encounter, and powerful people like Rich Veras and that kind of thing it is easy to fall into the "Yes, I agree, oh wow this is excellent this is the truth." I don't want to do that. That was the first concern I brought to Giussani. I want to draw from the Movement in the honesty of the experience that is proposed to me. I want a serious presentation of what the experience is like including its effective dimension even its sentimental dimension. Yes, even its sentimental dimension, but not depending on this at all because what makes it so is not all of these side perhaps nice-looking packages. It depends on what's inside. What's inside is not another book but a change of judgment about reality on our part. Whether I like it or I don't like it. Whether it brings me joy and I jump around and call everybody and kiss them, and thank everyone in the Movement. Whether nothing happens, no feeling, even perhaps a little anger - not at everybody else, but pity at those in the Movement who are wrapped up in the sentimental bash. Maybe a little anger. Anger at what? Anger at Christ that would want to play such games with me. Anger that would awaken such hopes by making me find a fraternity like what I have found. I am proud to consider myself a son of Father Giussani. But making me find this towards the end of my life, showed me that the resentment was just show. Not a malicious one but that it was just emotion? I began to be even a little bit angry. The removal, the setting aside, of whatever theological knowledge I had in order to try out what Father Giussani was trying to teach me, was done because I knew that it was a fuller knowledge. I set this anger aside because it led to amazement and for other reasons, it included the heart; the desires of the heart. The decision to try that out was a costly decision but it was a decision that I made willingly. Why? Because I am very saintly? No, because what is at stake is my ass! The future of my ass. I accepted it, and it has been the story of my last five years. One after one, the theological certainties still remain but they are being accompanied, or supplemented, or set aside, so that I can deal with the theological concepts at the level of the experience of my heart.

And let me tell you there are some moments when you are ecstatic, and you are so happy you want to run down the streets with joy! But there are other moments when you cannot stop crying. In his Easter message, the pope goes into this meditation about the candle.

He was talking about light, the new creation, God says again let there be light to banish the darkness that was overcoming the original creation's light. Beautiful material, beautiful stuff, and he almost finished the homily when he says that he has one more thing to tell us. In the liturgy of the vigil there is the reality of the Pascal candle and that the light that God emits is how the ceremony starts. Lumen Christi. The pope is saying that God's light illumines and gives you the new experience of seeing the newness of life. It allows you to see reality as it is in its original beauty. That light restores in us some experience of the beauty of creation itself. At the same time, remember, at what cost does that light shine? At what cost does that light bring about this new vision of the beauty of the new creation? The light shines at the cost of dying because as the fire burns the candle dies. Oh yes, the knowledge that you can get is awesome but sometimes it burns your heart away. Something like that I will listen to because I can't imagine a single greeting card containing that thought. Everything else I become suspicious of. Yeah, you met Jesus? Well, give him my regards. So, Julian Carrón spoke at the CL Easter vigil assembly, with the man who actually gave the retreat, Don Ezio Parato. He did it very much with Carrón. The assemblies are done together and even in the lessons Carrón has inserts in it that are lengthier than the usual ones. You can see it's an interesting common job. And it's interesting also to find someone new that I didn't know because its a whole set of new experiences and such that he gives witness to that is great. And one of them is the strength to which the arguments I've just made here. It's even stronger than the one I made. He spoke about the dangers of a purely philosophical or theological knowledge and the need for a knowledge that has the integrity of reason. You don't want a cheap Pascal candle but one that has the integrity and solidity of reason that gives light only when it burns away. That is awesome and that I want to listen to. We can use the category of event in order to understand better the newness in the new creation. This is something upon which I can embrace as containing the full truth of my life. I can adhere to this unreservedly until the end. Within this event lies my vocation to the priesthood which is my form of being a Christian and of following Christ. In following this path I came to the conclusion that there are many ways of following Christ. Of course there are, but this is the way in which he has chosen for me whether I like it or not. As we heard last night, it's nothing of what I expected it to be. Even the first year of my priestly life was not what I expected, and yet it has been fun, crazy, and Forest Gump-like, but on the other hand this is much more serious now. Two other possible dangers. Again, we need to concentrate on the category of event as an experiential category because that's what we're going to do. We are going to do this not just simply as a cold intellectual exercise, although that is necessary for the solidity of the other one which is in danger of becoming some kind of emotionalism. So, seeking to remove that emotional possibility, let us look at what really is happening when I am in that train station, and I hear my name pronounced, and I rejoice when I look and see it's you! It is you. Your voice. For a moment I thought, "No it can't be, it can't be old Sally." I thought it sounded like you, but I said, "Well it can't be. She can't have the same voice, but it is you. I thought you were dead. I thought you had migrated to some desert somewhere. I mean, I thought you had become a contemplative nun and here you are in Grand Central. This is so unbelievable." As they talk like that, as they look at each other like that, they're going to miss the train. But who cares? I'll miss the damn train, this is far more urgent and more important. More important except if your wife is waiting for you at the train station. Then you will have a little problem there. But for the moment the surprise is amazement. You want to make sure that the person is old Sally, just as you have made sure the candle is reasonable, and that it has solidity. This is indeed Sally, even though there are certain aspects of her face that have been marred by age, but still. Hey, more to play around with. This is still Sally, the old unshakable Sally. And you're here, and you remembered me. You remember I am sure. Everything we've done together! Here I am 71 years old and trying to fight my way through Grand Central to catch the train. Suddenly there is Sally. Now you must have experienced something like that. The question I ask you is: are you prepared to dismiss it at all as emotionalism, or did you grasp something? Did you learn anything? Was something new present there that passes the test of reason? Something that far exceeds the limitation of what today is considered reasonable? Like the first question that our friend asked me: is science the best way to transmit love? I told you this story. No, obviously it isn't. I mean it sounded like a joke, and it was an attempt at a joke, but I was serious when I said I didn't pursue someone to love or maybe even eventually marry by sending her solutions to problems for turning partial differential equations into unknowns. It's just so ridiculous. But what is the language then? I mean what do you say? Do you just be polite and say "You are my destiny?" -provided you don't drop dead first. Which I have no assurance of, oh no. Whoever is my destiny, I must be sure that she will be at that destiny when I arrive. I have a reasonable experience that will maybe make me sound silly. It will make me sound silly to stand up and say Christianity is an event. I say it with full awareness that it may make me sound silly, but I have no other way of saying it. This is the closest to what happens in my heart. An event is the sudden unexpected occurrence that awakens me to a presence. An event that awakens me to the presence of someone, the full one, or a part, or a group, but ultimately to a presence that is an event. And the proposal is that Christianity today must be presented within the category of an event. It must be presented as something that occurs. Something that happens, and that puts you into the presence of someone that changes the way you think. Someone who changes the way you see, and the way you act. Whether you are coherent or not in your actions, it is the way you know that this is the right way to act. That's the proposal about event.

If the proposal continues, one of the great advantages of this new garment for the Christian proposal, the event garment. The proposal is of course the same. The gospel is the same, Jesus is the same; the alpha and the omega. I am not proposing anything new; I am trying to present the gospel in the same way we saw at the mass yesterday. Peter and what's his name cure the paralytic. That's all they had and they presented it as one and all. Health for this man. But they could have said, wait here I forgot my wallet. I'll be back. I need to give you something that would help your immediate need. But no, this was an amazing response. So whether it was an amazing response or not, the category of event awakens interest in something that happens. You mean something happened to you? What happened to you? Oh I met a guru. Oh yeah, many people are turning east. I said no, I'm just an old skeptic at heart, but it can be very useful you know? To learn the eastern non-biblical religions because you know they're healthier. Judaism and Christianity keep you in a state of agitation all the time. The serenity of a Buddhist, that's fantastic. So I am glad that that was a great event, and that you met this person. That was an event. And it led to this. And you tried to wake him, a person in this ecstatic condition, like we tried yesterday when a certain person here was found venerating the ashtray that's outside instead of doing his prayers. Let him speak if he wants to speak. Anyway, we had a problem with a cult developing around that thing that's out there, that ashtray. You could be in the midst of such a Buddhist tranquil cult, floating in peace. And I could come in and try to tell them, "Oh who are you going to vote for Romney or Obama?" Or, "What the hell is going on? Why couldn't we get anyone better?" Do you think they are going to pay attention to you and say, "Wait let me stop floating around. Let me discuss politics with this guy." Bullshit, you'll say just don't bother me. These kinds of questions are the kind of questions I am running away from as I become detached from this kind of world. Who the hell cares, look at the size of the cosmos, come on read a little Stephen Hawking, look at what we're talking about matter, anti-matter, multi-verse, the whole thing string theory, and does it matter? Who the hell are Romney and Obama? Who the hell are you in the midst of all of this? I want to join my interior self to it, and you have interrupted this process by asking me about this stupid election that in the cosmic way of things doesn't matter at all. Because in that scale of things, you don't matter at all either. So let us learn how to become part of the oneness of the cosmos. Though that's the real question. Why do I say that? Because of Carrón and the other priest making references to Father Giussani and to Pope Benedict XVI, insisting that this is a danger originated or even provoked by the concept of event, and that we must be alert to avoid it. We must be alert to using an event, of using an unforeseen, an unexpected, as an excuse to do absolutely nothing about your problems of life every day. Life is a network of plots, like Russian novels, or like some soap opera in which you have multiple plots going on and they begin as someone who was describing the movie Decalogue, all take place in the same thing. Or if you want a real funny version of that, you could see *California Suite*, but there the plots never come together. Or read *Aunt*

Julia and the Scriptwriter,[25] in which this man writes soap operas. Unfortunately his mind begins to go and characters from one soap opera begin to show up in the other soap operas, including the dead. Characters from plot six begin to suddenly show up in plot ten until the man has to be dragged away to some kind of asylum; it's hilarious. It has one of the most hilarious scenes in the world to which I can confirm, namely when Jesus fell off the cross during a theater presentation of his life, passion, and death. It was not a presentation of his resurrection because we don't find that interesting in the Hispanic world. What's interesting is his death, so this was the last number. In the big number the three kings were on Mount Calvary and everyone who had ever appeared in the whole spectacle was there. Jesus is on the cross, and the words come from the actor, "I am falling." People begin to hear it and from next to the cross Our Lady and Saint John begin to move back until the whole stage is empty. Now why don't they just at least pull the curtain down? People are beginning to cry and to be horrified. This is a new ending to the story! Oh my god the world is going to pull out their rosaries and their scapulars! They had always brought them to this show. They wouldn't go to the Good Friday liturgy at the parish but they'll come to the theater with their little statues to be blessed by the actor who plays Jesus. I mean, maybe a little evangelization is needed but what's there is funny. And finally, louder and louder "me caigo, me caigo" and no one does anything about

---

25 Llosa, Mario Vargas; Aunt Julia and the Scriptwriter; London, United Kingdom; Faber and Faber; 2015

it and finally you hear the noise "me cai, carajo". That has nothing to do with this, yes it does! There are situations of many plots and the idea of event can be used to describe and to clean through those. Life is like those shows in that it is a crisscrossing. The word in Italian and in Spanish for this is "trama." How would you translate that? The plot. Something like that; the plot. Well life, the plot of life, our daily life, our daily day is a very complicated intersection of plots.

You put on a show here, you put on a show there, and in fact one of the tasks of the day is to make sure you remember in which plot you are. So you don't treat a particular subject say as funny, when in reality the people involved in that plot are suffering. Or the other way around. Instead of laughing at their stories that are meant as a joke you start weeping, it's ridiculous. So we balance the act.

We try to recognize how to behave in this plot, the other plot, but life is like that. Giussani says here, it's going to stay like that. You cannot use the appeal to an event to say that all of that stuff is unimportant. What matters, what really is important, is the event. You are to set aside all those worries and problems and pay attention to the only drama that matters, la unica que cuenta, the event. Beg for it; spend your time asking Jesus to make himself present to you. As for the rest, those are passing things. They are ephemeral. This is called a reductive use. This is the terminology they use, a reductive use of the category of event. There are two misuses of event, and the first one is a reductive use we must be aware that although we insist that the event is the proper and best category to evangelize today, we must be aware of these two dangers and many other perhaps which is the advantage of things like meetings and assemblies and all of that, because you may see things that have not seen and so forth. The second possible misuse of the category of event, is the tendency we have to corrode almost everything we touch. You can use the concept of event in order to build up such drama that it becomes an obstacle to evangelization because that is not the way Jesus comes to us. That is precisely one of the points we want to make, that is not the way, only through dramatic times. There are stories in the Old Testament and even in Acts in which they are like a competition between one of our guys and some pagan somewhere, as to who can perform the greatest miracle. And, obviously we win. I don't remember if we ever lose, if we did I suppose we would turn it into a Psalm. Anyway the idea is to use the terminology of the reality of an event in a way that it designates something so spectacular, so powerful, so irresistible, that you know immediately this is mine. Like I think of, when did you first get your vocation? The example given here in the retreat is very good. Saint Paul, before falling off that damn horse or that blessed horse, lived his criteria of life. He was a walking living out of the law. Saint Paul's view of it anyway as a Pharisee. It was the law that defined his identity. When he says he was a man of the law, he doesn't simply mean he was a man dedicated to the enforcement of the law but that his existence was that call to enforce the law in his own life. When he met Christ, when he fell off the horse, simply one thing happened: he substituted Christ for the law. What the law had been for him, now Christ was. A process of education had to follow, but that's where he was going. In which Christ became the criteria for everything he saw and how he saw it and how he judged it and how he dealt with it and what advice he gave. Maybe some advice was wrong, but you knew it was not coming from his belief in self-expertise. You knew he was trying to work out the consequences of the event of Damascus. We don't have his answer, but we have John and Andrew remembering the hour; 4pm. There's a precision there. Now most of us don't have that. We don't have that 4pm, or 5pm. I can put mine actually to the occasion when Scola arranged my lunch with Giussani. That gives me more or less the hour, but it doesn't play. I'm not constantly thinking about it although I am now more recently than I was before. In any case, I cannot use event in order to indicate something spectacular; something with big precision. Event shows itself to be what I am looking for, the category I am looking for if it really shows itself as a change in judgment, in criteria of judgment. Remember then, I cannot separate the dramas of daily life, and put them all here as the messy life, and here as the event. I cannot do that. And secondly, I cannot say this is unimportant because it has no dramatic presentation. Those two we are warned about here as dangers that have been detected in our people.

.

CPSIA information can be obtained
at www.ICGtesting.com
Printed in the USA
BVHW042024300119
539070BV00004B/10/P